ONE BIG UNION

Reviewing the history of a big idea

On the publication of
The Making of the Labour Movement
Ron Todd

Two Lectures
Ken Coates
Tony Topham

Reviews
Royden Harrison
Jack Jones
Julie Lindsay
Jim Mortimer
Diana Warwick
Kenneth O. Morgan
Eric Hobsbawm
William McCarthy
Nina Fishman
Lewis Minkin
Geoffrey Stuttard
Geoffrey Goodman
Philip S. Bagwell
Denis Smyth
Walter Greendale
Michael Barratt Brown

SPOKESMAN

First published in 2008 by
Spokesman
Russell House, Bulwell Lane
Nottingham
NG6 0BT
Phone 0115 9708381 Fax 0115 9420433
elfeuro@compuserve.com
www.spokesmanbooks.com

ISBN 978 0 85124 752 6
A CIP Catalogue is available fron the British Library.

Printed by the Russell Press Ltd., (phone 0115 9784505)
www.russellpress.com

CONTENTS

The Making of the Union

Ron Todd

Excerpts from Ron Todd's Foreword to The History of the Transport and General Workers' Union *by Ken Coates and Tony Topham.*

... In a sense, the TGWU was never born – it was made by hard labour, by incessant struggle, a monumental achievement that was at risk time and again. The authors have argued strongly for the essential continuity of the movement for amalgamation from the 1870s, through the great dock strike and up until the Leamington Conference of 1921. They argue that the unskilled workers that built the general labourers' unions were people of invention and imagination, setting trends with new forms of organisation and policy and strategy for the whole Labour movement. That is a different picture to the common one of unskilled labourers somehow 'catching up' with the pre-existing craft-union traditions, and then taking their due place in an established Labour movement. What these workers did was revolutionise this very movement, not least in its political aspirations, seen in the creation of the ILP and the Labour Party and the turn away from dependence on the Liberals; and also in their willingness to join with pioneer socialist thinkers and agitators when others sought respectable incorporation.

The labourers fashioned the unique multi-industrial structure of the eventual TGWU, going beyond federation to organisational unity, but keeping the proper autonomy of trade-group interests against a divisive sectionalism. They consistently demanded recognition and institutionalised bargaining machinery from employers and the state, long before they were achieved, amidst competing pressures for immediate gains in wages and conditions, the heady temptation of utopian independence, and moderation and subordination to the employers. The distinct strategy of securing independent trade unionism through joint regulation remains a strength to this day, a feature of mainstream trade unionism that politicians too often ignore in their attacks on trade-union power.

The authors portray leaders who were quick in the fields of building international trade unionism, especially in the transport industries, as a power-base for spreading their influence. Their 'new unionism' gave birth to the movement for independent labour representation, with the two dockers' unions and the Amalgamated Society of Railway Servants jointly convening the first union conference for forming labour's own political party.

Above all, the authors show how the pioneers were people of vision, capable of setting big targets and sustaining them in bad times as well as good. So it is a story of big thinking, rooted in bread-and-butter organisation, professional skills and political vision, in committed energy and incessant hard work.

It is a long time back, but it may be the case that some of the problems we face in the British trade union movement today are not so far removed from those covered in this first part of our history, least of all in the battle between the new unionism of today's TGWU and the various types of new realism espoused by some other trade unions.

We have been looking to extend our base by organising amongst the new army of part-time and temporary workers, the so called 'periphery' of the modern labour market, now totalling around a quarter of all workers. We have carried this and other important messages into the Labour Party at a time when there is a strong current of opinion in favour of a historic loosening of those very ties which came into being in the period which this history covers. We are seeking major mergers and looking to new kinds of links with European unions, below the formal levels already in existence, so that trade union solidarity can be developed, and common demands can be formulated, as close as possible to the factories and offices, as our economies become more deeply integrated. We have kept our focus wide, helping South Africa's oppressed workers to form their unions, and championing opposition to obscene militarism, when others have counselled a narrower focus on the immediate interests of employees, whatever they may be, and assuming that it is actually possible to separate the industrial and the political so neatly.

For organisations like ours, it has always made sense to examine where we have been, before asking where it is best to go now. I sense the end of a period and the opening of a new one. Not the end of working-class struggle and organisation; not the end of broad socialist aspiration; not the end of opposition to market forces and social domination by powerful classes who control and own the core capital of our societies; not the end of struggling against injustice and privileges secured through daily control of our society, often by subtle, but sometimes brutal means; not the end of independent trade unionism, rooted in workplace democracy, and its replacement by a carefully controlled system run by anonymous backroom committees and murmuring manipulators. No, I sense a renewal of emphasis on public interest, commonwealth and community, and on human decency undertaken as social obligation. A new and clear sense if what democracy is for ordinary people now that the Cold War competition about freedom is behind us.

I sense that a new era of international Labour movement organisation is near, most obviously in Europe and in what is fast becoming greater Europe. If there is to be a meaningful socialist party for the Europe of the future, then it must surely find its power and democracy in partnership with an extended trade unionism. And I sense that the terrible burden of military expenditure in advanced and less developed countries alike will be overturned – if future generations play their politics correctly – by forces committed to overcoming the vast problem of world poverty and the ecological threat ...

The two lectures published here celebrate the publication of the history of the Transport & General Workers' Union. They show how the dream of its founders was the creation of 'One Big Union'. With the formation of *UNITE the Union*, the realisation of that dream is brought that much closer. UNITE brings together people working in diverse occupations and locations, as did the founders of the T&G themselves all those years ago. In this booklet, Ken Coates and Tony Topham tell some of that story. For their full account, it is necessary, as the reviewers urge, to read *The Making of the Labour Movement*.

With grateful acknowledgements to Jim Hunt, then Midlands Regional Secretary of the TGWU, and Dr Ian Sutton, then Head of Adult Education at the University of Nottingham, whose organisations jointly convened the study day on 22 June 1991 at Nottingham University, when these lectures were given to an audience of trade union students.

From a Mob to a Movement

Ken Coates

Why bother with history? Why, above all, bother with one thousand pages of history which stops seventy years ago? Perhaps the best way to approach that is to try to draw for you a picture of what the allegedly unskilled workers, who gave us our subject matter, were like. How did they live, in the forgotten corners of Victorian Britain?

The fact of the matter is that in all British industrial towns, and above all, in the port cities, life was hell for the poorest people. It was calculated by sociologists, at the end of the century, that approximately one-third of the population of London was living in poverty, and by poverty they did not mean what modern sociologists mean. They meant dire and suffocating squalor. Poverty meant tenements in which sometimes five or ten people lived in one room. It meant courtyards where the water supply, such as it was, was shared between many such households. It meant privies that had to be emptied by the night soil man. London, for instance, in the last days at the end of nineteenth century Britain, had a whole tract of housing in the East End which was, as William Blake and Cobbett used to say in earlier days, 'a wen'. I am reminded of modern China when I look at those discrepancies between wealth and poverty. The West End, home of the lords of the earth, the owners of empire, people of unparalleled riches and ostentation, lay on one side. On the other was the East End crawling with vice, terrified by Jack the Ripper, an horrendous stew.

And what happened in those straitened circumstances? People normally have a certain capacity for supporting one another. People can normally be kindly, friendly and helpful, and there was, among these particular people, every need for all those resources of solidarity and decency, which the poorest of them could muster. But also, when one is competing for life, there are many instincts which pit people against each other. It can be a brutal struggle, each against all, for survival of those who are miscalled the fittest, which often means survival of the less conscientious and the least moral in the deprived population. All these things were mixed together; base and pure, mean and generous to a fault.

We do not try in this book to give you an idealised picture. Instead we try to recover the feel of those communities. The docks grew up in cities which had exploded in size, because the rail networks were decanting people into these vital areas at a rate far faster than the cities themselves could grow to assimilate them. Many or most of the people who were sucked into these growing urban areas were agricultural people. I have always thought it is a libel to say that such people were unskilled, but they had skills from a previous age. That is why so many of them became carters, because they knew about horses. Many others became dockers: many swapped roles, and many of the country people who did not actually migrate would find themselves drawn into the town after the harvest was in, which was when unemployment hit the agricultural labourers. Nearly always the docks had far more people wanting to work than could normally be given work. There were just rare moments when the weather was right, when the winds were right, when the demand was right, when the ships lined up to unload, that you could have something which fleetingly resembled full employment. Normally this was not so.

Work was organised quite differently in such places from the orderly rhythms we came to expect later in the car factories, which are so well understood and well remembered in the Midlands. The industrial discipline of this population that we are talking about hardly existed. People had come from the land, they had not become inured to the routine of the hooter and the clock, still less the drill of time study and careful managerial control. They queued up outside the dock gates and fought to get in. The foreman picked the fittest and set them on. The rest were sent away. They would go hungry.

So what are we talking about? Why have I gone into all this? I have gone into it because I want you to understand that everything that we take for granted today about trade unions was still unformed, unfixed: everything. We take for granted that there are and have always been working class people. But in a sense, in those days, these were not such working class people. Then, in the docks, there was a mob, when it all got together: and when it was not together there were tens of thousands of miserable individuals normally ground down into isolation, loneliness and poverty. Yet somehow or other those same people became a collective which was not a mob, no longer a bunch of social atoms either. They became something which today everybody assumes has always been with us, an independent-minded working class, with a self-confident working class movement. Banding those previously forlorn people together was actually the major breakthrough which created modern British democracy.

I know in school we were told it all started with the Magna Carta,

1215 and I don't know what. But actually at the time we are speaking about, the very large majority of British people had no say whatever about who were to become the politicians who might lead them. All women lacked the vote, but very large numbers of men also lacked the vote. There had been a big electoral reform in 1884, and the working class electorate had been increased. But it depended on various complex qualifications, according to household tenure, and there was the additional problem that middle class people commonly had two votes, because they could vote where they lived, and they could also vote where they held business property. That meant that you could not just take the electorate and do the sums and work out what the entitlement to political involvement was. And that is why, in the words of the old song,

> *'Every little Briton who's ever born alive,*
> *is either a little Liberal or a little Conservative.'*

The prosperous classes monopolised the vote. When you shared a tenement room in East London with all those other families, you lived in a world where things like voting could hardly be imagined.

And then suddenly, something happens. We see the outcast people associating themselves. Ben Tillett is one of the great heroes in this story, and what Ben Tillett says he did is very revealing. When he started work on the docks, having been a seaman, he took upon himself a stigma which made it impossible to confess where he was actually employed. Outside his work, when he was mixing in 'society', he would try to conceal what his job was. People who were doing his job were universally described as 'dock rats'. Ben Tillett claimed that he himself was the man who invented the word 'docker', which description marked a new beginning. It gave both self-repect and, yes, status to the job. But why were they seen, and why did they see themselves, as 'dock rats'? Because in order to get work, in attending the call-on, which was the selection of the fittest men to work those ships that were available for working, the men had, quite normally, to fight each other to be chosen. It was a raw, physical battle. There were innumerable descriptions of it, including lots by sociologists who began to visit and report at the time. It was a war. People's coats (and, said Tillett, sometimes even their ears) were torn off in the struggle to get to the gate and earn the pittance which was the difference between starvation – there was no welfare state – and a meagre livelihood. Sometimes men would be injured and maimed in the battle. All sorts of attempts were made to organise these people, and we have gone through those events in the book.

At the end of the 1880s, however, this whole submerged population exploded in a great rage of rebellion. It was started by the matchgirls who worked in Bryant and May's factory in Bow. They rebelled because they were levied a penny a week contribution, a compulsory tax put on them by the employer, an important Liberal, who demonstrated his Party loyalty by building a statue of Gladstone, at the girls' expense, outside the factory. The girls were enraged by this, and in fact they mutinied when the statue was unveiled. There was a mob scene, when the girls threw themselves on the statue, and actually it got covered in blood where they had been beating it with their bare hands. So enraged were they all about the forced deduction of money to sustain a political cause which, they felt, had nothing to do with them. And yet it surely did have something to do with them, because they were the most exploited and suffocated group of people that you could ever meet. We have a picture of them in our book. Little waifs, they were, and they got all kinds of industrial diseases, including the dreadful malady, 'phossy jaw', from the phosphorus used in the matches they made. This melts the bones. One of these children appeared in the House of Commons when the final strike broke out, and took her headscarf off, to the astonishment of the MPs, because all her hair had fallen out. Actually, that was the least of the problems, and many worse things than that happened. But that glimpse of Hell so shattered the MPs that they all declared themselves in support of the matchgirls. And when the East End of London was hit by this unlikely strike, it caused a tremendous amount of public concern. The truth about poverty and exploitation became momentarily visible to more comfortable people. That lit a fire which spread out, so that there was a huge conflagration among first, the gasworkers, and then, the dockers. This was the movement which generated the great dock strike of 1889.

That dock strike was a fantastic event. It mobilised a hundred thousand people of East London, the poorest people not only on the docks, but all around them. They paraded through London day after day after day, and as they made their processions their grievances were paraded in the press. We had, in 1889, just entered the beginning of the age of the modern popular press, so those grievances presented themselves all over the country. So, indeed, did their rebellion. Suddenly you could see the poorest of the nation marching together and insisting that their complaints should he heard. In this way, all over the country, the dock strike was seen as a flame of rage and indignation, and of protest and hope. And now what did that do?

In history there are many examples of similar outbreaks, in which oppressed people have risen up and asserted themselves: and there are many of these examples – I could cite the history of some of the great strikes of the American labour movement, when after a year had gone by you could go back to see where that rebellion had been and find not a trace left of it. Nothing. People had vented their anger and then sunk back into quiescence.

But what the London dockers did was more than to rebel. They set out to create a union and to demand negotiations between the dockers and the port employers. A variety of other material demands were concerned: they are all recorded in the book. But all of them involved a new and central demand for recognition.

Recognition is the magic word. Its achievement, over time, did not just bring about collective bargaining: it also brought with it modern democracy. And that is why we must ask, what does recognition mean? There you had among the dock employers the most disreputable bunch of old feudal magnates that ever there was. They really were money-grubbing, grasping, backward-looking monsters. Against this grouping, the dockers' union, with the help of the Catholic Church in the person of Cardinal Manning, with the help of parts of the Liberal establishment, and with the help of the liberal press, notably the evening paper in London, *The Star*, managed to create such a pressure that even these, the most backward employers in the land, were compelled to negotiate. They were compelled to recognise that these workmen were no longer individual 'dock rats'. Now they were the Dockers' Union. You see what that means: first of all, it means the dockers had won their claims; secondly, it means the dockers could build their organisation; thirdly, and this is the key question, it means that the dockers could recognise their own unity, their community of interest, through its reflection in the eyes of their enemy. He *recognised* them. Their basic wage and conditions, then, came to depend upon their adversary's recognition that they had been agreed with the union.

So the men were a unity. I think that is a core element in the creation of modern democracy, because it meant that the poor, once they got the idea of union into their heads, even if the recognition was later taken away, had already experienced what was to become crucial to them: the knowledge that their individual strength would inevitably be the greater when they belonged to a collective in which they had confidence and trust. That is the basis upon which they began to organise, not only collective bargaining in industry, but also the long and difficult process which led to political representation.

Of course, political action became necessary because the people who were 'recognised' were a minority of the great population outside, clamouring for work. Although you could try to organise similar recognition for that wider population, and perhaps win many successes, it was a bit like baling out the ocean with a spoon. To make a substantial change, extending recognition to all who needed it, you had to get political representation and you had to get the vote. But to use that vote you had also to win a second recognition, expressing your own special political interests in distinction to those of the existing parties, representing the comfortable classes.

It wasn't an accident that the girls in Bryant and Mays rebelled about the statue of Gladstone. The Liberal employers were among the most persistent of all in exploiting the un-unionised labour forces and in driving down conditions. The same thing was the case in Brunner Mond, the forerunners of ICI; in one of our chapters we describe how Tom Mann became involved in a big effort to impose shorter hours and safe conditions in that enterprise. He had to adopt an alias, and smuggle himself into employment, so keen were these employers to keep out unions and all who might advance them.

Voting Liberal, then, which was what such working class voters as there were were most commonly wont to do, was not going to advance their interests at work, because the same Liberals who stood on the hustings promising all kinds of benevolence were also the big employers who resisted unions. So there grew up a campaign for separate labour representation. Recognition, representation, these are all parts of the creation of an identity. It wasn't already there: it had to be made, it had to be built.

Of course, what happened was that the dock strike led directly to the election of the first really independent Labour MP, Keir Hardie, Member for West Ham, and also to the election of John Burns, who had played a key role in 1889, and of Havelock Wilson, the Seamens' leader. These political events arose directly from the organisation of the dockers and the surrounding transport and general workers, the gas workers, the people involved as carters and all the rest of them.

In turn, organisation led directly into local government representation, with the winning of Labour voices on the new local councils, first of all in the London area and then further afield. When

Keir Hardie was elected, although he was not a docker, he became the political representative of the dockers' new unionism, and he was directly supported by the leaders of that process. Keir Hardie was elected three years after the great dock strike.

The year after that, in 1893, there met the first conference of the Independent Labour Party. It was called in Bradford. Who was the Parliamentary candidate of the ILP in Bradford? Who but our old friend Ben Tillett! Very soon afterwards, Tom Mann was selected as the Independent Labour candidate in Halifax.

When you ask why, what you find is that in Bradford, too, they had an immense strike, the Manningham Mills dispute. It had been caused by contraction in the textile industry resulting from trade protection in the United States. That strike itself created an enormous popular unity and rebellion in Bradford, but the Bradford people, including their leaders, looked towards the dockers' leaders, because those dockers' leaders had been advertised all over the country as near miracle-workers. These, after all, were the people who had turned the people of the East End from a lethargic and dispersed mass of individuals into a united fighting force. So, send for Ben Tillett, send for Tom Mann! And up they came to Yorkshire. Who better to choose as parliamentary candidates? But we should notice that they, too, were the people who sharpened the argument so that the ILP was actually begun, and within one year, Tom Mann, who was the dockers' President, had also become the General Secretary of the ILP.

I want to make it very plain that it was the struggle of these same leaders of the transport workers, which persuaded the TUC itself to go for shorter working hours by law, in the campaign for the legal eight hour day. This we still have not won. But it was these leaders who prepared the ground for the formation of the political Labour Party, the party we know today, and a key issue in that argument was that of working time. Shorter hours by law were not what Liberal employers wanted. So, in Parliament, they voted against. Everyone could then see what limits there were to liberal philanthropy.

At the turn of the century, it was the Liverpool dockers' leader, James Sexton, and the London dockers' leader, Ben Tillett, who joined forces with the railwaymen's union, to put down proposals at the TUC in 1899, ten years after the story began, to convene the conference which founded the Labour Party. Those three organisations met to composite their separate resolutions into a joint motion, under the chairmanship of Keir Hardie. This was then carried through the TUC, so that the conference that called the Labour Party into being was two-thirds the responsibility of the Transport and General Workers' forerunners, and one-third the responsibility of their allies in what later became the NUR.

Now why? The answer is that this political struggle was absolutely essential for the poorest people, because they lacked the monopoly position of skilled workers. They could not trade on their scarcity. Instead they had to secure some political intervention to make space for recognition.

Recognition was reinforced by government intervention, by the government holding the ring in industrial relations between the two sides. The government indeed made very tentative interventions in this process throughout the first part of this century. As time wore on, it made more and more strong appearances, culminating in a rush of government actions establishing a powerful presence during the First World War. But each intervention reinforced recognition, and therefore reinforced the sense of identity that workers got from seeing their unity reflected in the adversary's eyes. That is what made possible what happened after the First World War, the displacement of the Liberal Party by a Labour opposition led by Ramsay MacDonald.

None of that would have happened if there had been no successful move to organise the so-called unskilled workers. And all of it was a direct result of what? Of the inventive skills of these same dispossessed people.

The transport workers did not follow lamely behind the skilled workers, the aristocrats of labour. At the beginning of the trade union story, if you remember, there were some skilled workers' unions in which you would be fined for not going to the meeting. There were others in which you were not allowed into the meeting if you did not wear a tall silk hat, and a frock coat, and a bow tie. I am not exaggerating. The rules used to state you had to be 'properly dressed'. To be properly dressed, of course, cost an arm and a leg. When the first dockers' union delegates went to the TUC, there was a famous row because John Burns, that great spokesman of the dock strike who was elected as an MP in 1892, wrote an article in which he pointed out that the skilled workers were not only better turned out, but also all taller, stouter, better built, and smoother than these ragged individuals who now came in representing the dockers. Burns was accused of something close to racialism for saying this, but it was the sober truth.

As these people organised themselves, all their skills and all their inventiveness found an outlet. They were making and shaping a political process. That process led to the formation of the Labour Party, and it also led to the extension of the franchise. This became unavoidable during the First World War, because millions of voteless men were mown down to save 'their country'.

After conscription came in, it could not even be said they were volunteers. Clearly it was indefensible to be herded into war and slaughter without the right to vote on whether to support the hostilities or not. The call for male suffrage led to the universal franchise in which women were able to vote, and in which general elections could begin to register the actual opinions of the British population. And the first time that that happened was in the period immediately after the First World War. That is the date of British modern democracy, and you can say really that the whole of that process is covered in our book, and that there was, in fact, at the beginning of the story, no political democracy in this country, there was a club of the oligarchs, and at the end of the story rudimentary popular democracy was beginning to assert itself, and the people were beginning to find a way to express themselves.

At the forefront of that popular movement were the so-called unskilled workers, the lesser breeds, the ones with dirty hands, the ones who could not dress in the proper attire, the ones who were outside the pale. That's an extraordinary story!

People should be very proud of the traditions of this trade union. It is really the uncelebrated story of everything that is good in Britain. The last thing I should say is that in the processes which led to all these developments, there was a very important juncture.

You see, when you began to organise against the indifference and hostility of an enfranchised minority, you had to look which way you could go in order to express the democratic will, and among the people who joined the dockers' union the day after the great dock strike were two branches in Sweden, another branch in Holland. What were they doing? Port workers everywhere had the same interests. Seamen everywhere had the same interests. From the beginning, they saw their interests as involving a linkage, like with like. The workers had no country. They really did not have a country, they could not vote where they lived, they had no power there: but they had a common interest with other workers doing the same jobs that they were doing in another country, in which they, too, could not vote. Furthermore, if they all stood together, they could prevail, because they could impose recognition on all the employers in all the ports around the globe. The dockers during the dock strike would have been starved back to work if it had not been for the raising of tens of thousands of pounds by Australian trade unionists. This gave the impulse to an enormous movement of international support and solidarity.

What we tend not to see is that it also was a choice: were you going to organise nationally? In that case you had to organise a political party, and you had to win the vote. To cap that, you then had to win the electorate, and you then had to go through all the political processes you understand. Or were you going to organise internationally? In that case you could create brand new institutions, because there wasn't any international parliament. So you could 'do it yourself' by assembling an overwhelming force, which would mean that people would have to listen to the voices that you represented.

There was a long struggle between these two roads to democracy. It was finally resolved when the governments of Western Europe gave in to popular pressure and conceded the popular vote. To make this happen it took a world war in which millions of people were killed.

Our story has been completely different since then, because in every country, and above all in Britain, once we got the vote it meant that our main way forward was national, because we could organise, we could win elections, we could put people in the government, we could change the policy. Obviously common sense said that you combine collective bargaining and political mobilisation, and on the national plane that was your way forward. Of course, now we are coming round in a circle, because at the national plane we find we do all these things, and we win an election, and yet still we can't change anything, because all the industrial forces have now become international themselves, and they confront us with the kind of power that our unions never had, but that they were seeking to get, back at the end of the nineteenth century. They confront us with immense power, and we shan't win it back until we unite our forces at least as closely in order to be able to bargain for the people that we represent, whether they live in Sicily or in Denmark or in Birmingham. That's a new agenda, a really powerful agenda, but it's an agenda which I think you get enormous help in meeting if you work through the experiences of our grandfathers and great-grandfathers in the story that we've been trying to tell. There is nothing new under the sun. Actually, this history is as much about tomorrow as it is about yesterday.

Unity in Diversity

Tony Topham

I want to say a word of appreciation for the Union's role in promoting this history. They have given Ken and me and the whole project (Nottingham University specifically), every support, both material and moral, and in terms of access. In the words of the old Workers' Control slogan, the union has 'opened all the books' to us, without restraint; they have not sought to tell us how to write the history. Indeed Ron Todd said precisely: 'We want it warts and all'. There are a few warts, but they do not disfigure the face of this union.

Why the history? Why the history of labour, why the history of the T&G particularly? It seems to me always in trade union work that a grasp of history, an understanding of where we come from and what we inherit, is essential if we are to have guides and compasses and maps to take us from where we are to where we want to be. And the elimination of history by authority, the elimination of *people's* history, the common people's history, is a source of some worry when it is written out of the curriculum. Every dominant class in history has always tried to suppress the collective memory of those whom it has sought to dominate.

When the Jacobite rebellion in eighteenth century Scotland was put down by the English army, the Highland Scots were forbidden to speak the Gaelic language, they were forbidden to wear the kilt. What was going on there was an attempt to sever a people from its history, from a history from which they could derive pride and a sense of community.

Today, we do not have such draconian laws as those administered by the English in the Highlands, but we do have a tendency for a kind of self-censorship to operate in some of the media. In 1889, the Great Dock Strike in London was one of the high points of the history we have been studying. 1989 was its centenary, and I and many others became increasingly conscious, as 1987 and 1988 went by, that preparations ought to be made for a serious examination and appraisal of one of the most important moments in modern British history, in the mass media.* I spoke (I shall be accused of name-dropping) to good socialist dramatists like Alan Plater and Trevor

*The Union did, of course, publish a beautiful illustrated book, *The Great Dock Strike, 1889,* in 1989, to mark the centenary.

Griffiths, and they said to me: 'Well, we'll try, but we don't think there's a hope of any producer taking this up and treating it seriously'. I am naïve enough to find that shocking, especially when set against the amount of space given over in 1988 to the celebration of the tercentenary of the so-called 'Glorious Revolution' of 1688, with Mrs. Thatcher leading the chorus of sheer baloney which claimed that event as the foundation of democracy in Britain. We cannot reach the mass media, but our History is an attempt to recover your history for your appraisal and your understanding. It is not done in any spirit of nostalgia; we hope it will be used as an active tool for shaping your thoughts, your policies, your future.

Between us we have got a difficult job to try and summarise what, as you see, are two rather large books of nearly one thousand pages. Indeed, at the end of it we have only reached 1922, and the moment when, formally and legally, the T&G acquired its title and began its life. We had agreed at the beginning of the project that we would have a preliminary chapter on what we called the pre-history of the union, the dockers' strike 'and all that'. But as we began to look at it more carefully, we found that we needed a far deeper explanation than was possible in a chapter, of the extraordinary, unique nature of the amalgamation process which produced the TGWU. We needed to understand the origins and the roots of the eighteen unions which came together in 1922, because we began to discover, in looking at the amalgamation debates, that those people were drawing on what they themselves understood as a long tradition, a powerful tradition, a powerful set of values, and we were drawn ever further backwards to the rudimentary port unions of the 1870s.

We also found the existing accounts of 1922 too cold. We did not find in them the excitement that we ourselves discovered in looking at the original sources, the minutes, the debates, the conference reports, and the personal memoirs. We also found it was quite inadequate to say that Ernest Bevin did it overnight. Ernest Bevin comes well, I think, out of our studies, and it is no denigration of his role to say that he himself was the inheritor of a long tradition, which he felt and understood with great sensitivity. That does not prevent us appreciating his organising genius in bringing the thing to fruition.

We uncovered many unread sources in Transport House and elsewhere. We found that other historians had blazed a trail for us with a series of very valuable regional histories, and the whole thing was crying out to be pulled together. We wanted to say, too, that here was a *single* span of history connecting, in an unbroken arch, the very earliest aspirations of so-called 'unskilled' labourers', dockers', and carters' unions, with the amalgamation of 1922. We did not want to see it broken up into artificial and unreal sections of history; it is one history, one arch. When we saw the significance of that point, we understood that what we were looking at also was not just the emergence of the structural unity of the TGWU, we were looking at 'The Emergence of the Labour Movement' itself.

I want to say a few words about structural questions, and to examine why the slogan 'One Big Union' was present at all the dozens and dozens, perhaps hundreds, of amalgamation mass rallies and meetings which the Provisional Executive called across the country in 1921, to put the case for the unity of eighteen unions and to win the members' ballots – for they had to ballot for the amalgamation. Wherever they went they displayed that slogan, 'One Big Union', and that is the question that I largely want to address. *Why was that so?*

The other reason why we wanted to write this pre-history was that we found that it was *our* unions, the unions *we* were studying, which were making the pace, and we found ourselves disagreeing with those historians who have said: 'Oh, yes, there *was* such a thing as New Unionism, the dock strike and all that, in the late 1880s, but it was either wiped out in the ensuing slump, or it moderated its radicalism and was absorbed into the older routines and norms of the pre-socialist craft union-dominated TUC of the 1860s-1870s'. We found, on the contrary, that our unions were consistently making the pace and transforming the movement. We also had, or came to have, a strong instinct to write, or in some cases to rewrite, the record of the individuals who took part in the process we have tried to describe. Some of these names will be familiar to you – Ben Tillett, Tom Mann, John Burns, Jimmy Sexton of the Liverpool dockers, Ernest Bevin of course, Harry Gosling of the London Lightermen. But Bob Williams went down history's memory hole, and I think we have pulled him out of it. He was the secretary of the Transport Workers' Federation, which was the essential predecessor of the Transport Workers' Union, and he was a towering influence. Connolly and Larkin, two great Irish thinkers and activists, contributed more than a little to our story; all of these people we found to be bold, original thinkers, many of them with the gift for words. Many of them have left their written memoirs for us, which we have used extensively, to allow them to speak for themselves wherever possible.

The practice of those times included rather more *glasnost* than there is today. The practice was to print and publish the minutes, the verbatim records of all conferences and congresses and annual meetings, from the record of the shorthand typist. They printed the lot, and we have found that those records bring history to life. Far from being dry as dust, it is like recreating a continuous drama, to re-read them and then to distil them into our account. There is a whole string of secondary characters, and I hope you read the book, and I hope you come to know them all as we came to know them, as we were working.

These are the reasons why we had to do this book. As Rod Todd wryly reports in his Foreword: 'Well, it didn't turn out quite as we expected it', and that was true for Ken and me as well. You will judge whether we got it right.

Let me turn to the structure question. George Woodcock was the TUC General Secretary who, in the early 1960s, said rather pedantically, in the course of a TUC debate (one of those perennial debates that we have about reorganising the structure of British trade unionism): 'Structure is a function of purpose'. I thought I had long understood that, but I understood it much better after this four year study. The industrial *purpose* of the general and 'unskilled' and transport workers of 1870-1922 drove them always towards *structural* unity, the One Big Union goal.

What were those industrial purposes? First, there was the need to exclude all potential blacklegs from strike-breaking in the casual labour industries such as port transport. Almost from their birth, the unions that we have been looking at, although they might originate as dockers' unions or, in one case as a gas workers' union (that is the one that got away and became the General and Municipal Workers' Union!), added the subtitle '... and General Labourers' to their name. In other words, they were saying that the whole field of non-craft employment at least was open for their recruitment, because all non-unionists were potential blacklegs who would break their strikes. So immediately they went out to recruit agricultural workers, carters, in South Wales the tinplate men, factory and mill labourers everywhere. So that was one clear purpose, to provide the widest possible cover.

The second purpose was to overcome sectionalism. There is a great deal about sectionalism in our book, not as an 'ism', but as a living story of particular occupations and territories and areas of organisation, which are not simply to be despised for their narrowness. Sectionalism in one sense is a derogatory term, and properly so, in trade unionism, but you have to understand where people come from, and the roots of their earliest loyalties. The lightermen of London, a great 'aristocracy of labour', with a long tradition, the stevedores who claimed all the ship-board work, the coaltrimmers of South Wales and the north-east coast, all had specialist occupations which were the source of their first experience of solidarity. Yet everyone who understood the weakness of general labour understood that sectionalism was not enough, that it had to be overcome. And the question of how to overcome it, how to create a structure in which people who, at work, were in sectional rivalry and often, very often, in conflict with one another, could live together, runs on throughout the period that this volume covers. Jimmy Sexton in his memoirs described the early Liverpool dockers' union in which the branches were tiny little clubs, each one representing an occupation and each one claiming superior social or industrial status over all others. That is what had to be countered, and the striving against it is an important part of our story.

Harry Gosling, who became the first President of the T&G, was the General Secretary of the Watermen and Lightermen of London on the Thames – very exclusive brethren, with very conservative craft instincts. But Harry was a New Unionist, seized by the gospel of unity in the years immediately following the London dock strike, and he became impatient with the conservative-minded attitudes of his members. He said to Tom Mann (who towers in this whole story, of course) on one occasion in the 1890s: 'I'm getting tired of them, Tom. Shall I leave them and come over to you?' – meaning 'come over' to the general, and generally aspiring, union of dock labourers. And Tom said: 'No, stay where you are, bring them along with you.' And Harry did, to the point when he was able to 'bring them along' into the amalgamation of 1922. Tom McCarthy, who was the stevedores' leader in London in 1889, and therefore a member of another port aristocracy, did leave. He left the Stevedores' Union and became a national organiser for the Dock, Wharf, Riverside and General Workers' Union, Ben Tillett's dockers' union. He also contested the West Hull Parliamentary seat, for the ILP, against the Liberal Party's candidate, Charles Wilson, the largest private ship-owner in the world, in 1895.

A man called George Jackson, who is, I suppose, quite an obscure character, was general secretary of the largest Northern union of Tramwaymen and Carters. (Somebody must, incidentally, write the full industrial history of the busmen and tramwaymen and carters of the North and Midlands.) George Jackson's Annual reports of the 1890s are full of it. 'I don't think we shall make any more progress', he said, 'with our sectional unions. We must find a wider unity. I don't know whether it will be a federation or an amalgamation, but eventually we've got to have One Big Union'. Now 'One Big Union' is historically associated with revolutionary aspirations, but George Jackson would have presented himself as a modest, pious, Christian aspirant for simple justice for his members.

How, then, do you overcome sectionalism? Certainly not by suppressing it, certainly not by denying its existence, because it will reassert itself, particularly in bad times. Our story goes over the booms and slumps of classic pattern, and the sectionalism of a little local group nursing a single occupation in a single dock reasserts itself each time that the dole queues lengthen. So you cannot simply suppress it, and the origin of the unique structure of your union, the TGWU, the Trade Group structure, lies in this understanding. I find that to be one of the most revealing and rewarding discoveries that we made. I repeat that this does not denigrate Bevin's role, but everyone has supposed that Bevin invented Trade Groups. He did not; he made them live, he brought them into a structure by sheer sweat and skill and organising ability in the amalgamation process itself. But Bevin inherited a discussion which had gone on since the 1890s. How do we harmonise diversity within unity? Answer: autonomous 'departments', (as they were called in the early days; 'Trade Groups' was the later name for them). And give those departments sufficient autonomy so that sectionalists will be persuaded to amalgamate, unfearful that they will lose their identity.

Parallel with sectionalism there is regionalism. Regionalism also has to be overcome. Bear in mind that many of the unions that we begin to study in the 1870s and 1880s had names like the Cardiff Coaltrimmers' Association, the London Stevedores' Society, the Halifax Carters' Union, the Bolton Carters' Union, the Huddersfield Tramway Union, the Liverpool Carters' Union, and on and on. And then of course there were the nationalisms, from which derived a rather powerful form of regionalism. The Scottish Dockers' Union, the Scottish Carters' Union, even (in a breakaway), the *North* of Scotland Carters' Union, and the Belfast Tramway Union, and the North Wales Quarrymen's Union. So geographical, communal loyalty formed another powerful bond, but not a bond which would achieve the purposes for which One Big Union and General Unionism were striving.

So we follow through, in our volume, the struggles to overcome regionalism. Once again, it cannot be overcome by suppressing it; again you have to adapt, and create a regional structure. We think we have said something in the volume about why many of the regional headquarters of the T&G today are still in the towns and locations where they were fixed in 1922, many in the major ports. Merseyside, which is in everyone's minds these days, because of its strong regional identity (to put it mildly!) is a very strong case in point. In 1921, Sexton's dockers in Liverpool did not turn out in sufficient numbers to win a ballot vote for the amalgamation, and Bevin and the rest were at great pains to press for a new ballot, and to bring those regionalists into the union. To do that, the carrot that they held out was a Regional Headquarters in Liverpool, and a separate Region was formed with a Liverpool Headquarters. Originally, the scheme had been to incorporate Merseyside in the Region based in Salford. You have reverted to that now, of course, as you know. But the Liverpudlians, the scouse, still insist on a divisional status within Region 6! The book is full of such intriguing continuities.

Perhaps the most extreme case is that of Hugh Lyon, who was the General Secretary of the Scottish Carters' Union. In the years of the First World War, national bargaining was emerging as a standard and effective practice, a great advance on tenuous local bargaining. It was especially important for carters who worked in local labour markets, which were isolated from one another. Hugh Lyon's union was persuaded to attend the first national bargaining sessions in Manchester. Having had a taste of it, he reverted sharply to his Scottish nationalism, persuading his union to pass a resolution saying that 'on no account are we to participate in anything which has its headquarters in any English town or region, nor to participate in any English bargaining'. That was regionalism of a special, nationalistic, kind. Hugh Lyon went one better, for he was also a sectionalist through to the end of his days; his executive forced him to retire in 1937, and his union did not come into the T&G until Alex Kitson brought it in, in the 1960s. That is how long Scottish nationalism survived there. But Hugh Lyon, up to 1937, could not really accept that a motorised lorry driver was a proper member of his union, because horsemen were his concern! That is nationalism and sectionalism compounded. The book is full of such studies and how they were overcome. And they make the case for autonomous regions within the T&G.

Today, everyone in Europe and in Westminster is thrashing around to discover the right federal constitution for the European Community (or how not to, as the case may be!) Our book is full of our people's creative, original endeavour to construct a constitution which would bond the whole together, whilst allowing the parts to express themselves.

Here, of course, I have to apologise, in a sense (it is the result of history) to Region 5 in the Midlands, because it is inevitable in the nature of Volume 1 that our main regional interests lie in the port and coastal areas: Glasgow, Liverpool, Hull, Manchester, the South Wales ports, Bristol, Southampton, London, Belfast and Dublin ...

The other purpose which strikes one very forcibly, and has struck one or two people who have given our book an early reading, is so obvious it seems hardly worth saying. A purpose that was fundamental for the new unions was *survival,* was continuity, was permanence. That sounds like a truism today, when very few unions get born and very few unions die, except through the process of merger. But we have found dozens and dozens, running certainly into hundreds of unions in the field that we cover, which have a spurt of life in the 1880s, 1890s, and then simply collapse and die. So continuity was by no means assured, and the constitution-makers and the organisers of our period had that object in mind all the time.

Now let me come to what is the largest purpose of all, which is the establishment of a recognised status as trade unions, recognition from the employers, with collective bargaining as the consequence, as the method for advancing the wages and conditions of all these people in this society. Ken elaborates on the social and political significance of 'recognition', on which we have, I think, some new thoughts. As for the industrial purpose, of course, this again sounds like a truism.

Of course, trade unions are about collective bargaining! But not all of them. And it was not always so. The craft unions' practice was to establish a District Rate by internal agreement, and to say to their members: 'You take that rate or none at all, move on, we don't need to bargain.' And that practice was going on in the Midlands even down to quite modern times, with the member responsible for negotiating the District Rate for himself, and being subject to union discipline if he took work below it.

Ernest Bevin linked structural unity and the power to negotiate very early on in his career in the then Transport Workers' Federation. They were debating our problem, union amalgamation, just before the First World War. Here again, let me just pause to underline the point on which I insist, that nothing just began to happen in 1922. In a major debate, between all the transport and general workers' unions in the country, on the eve of the First World War, Bevin comes along as a representative of the Bristol carters and Tillett's Dockers' Union and says this:

> 'I happen to be where the dockers and carters are in one union, in Bristol, and there the carters have been more successful than in any other town in the country in relation to the conditions they were under. I say it is the consciousness of the employer, the whole time that he is negotiating with the coaltrimmer, the docker, the carter, the seaman, that they have a central executive behind them representing the co-operation of their fellows in the same organisation that gives the power to negotiate. It is not so much a power to attack as a power to negotiate.'

That is a young man, and the greatest of them, from that second generation of leaders, expressing an early approximation, an early version of the formula which I stress. Obviously collective bargaining is both a method and a purpose. It is a method to achieve the purpose of the improvement and standardisation of wages and working conditions.

So a last word about what we might call 'methods'. The New Unions of the 1880s and again of course in 1911, with their renewal in the great labour unrest of those years, have been famous for their use of the strike weapon. Of course, and we have tried to celebrate in our text the verve and excitement and drama and achievement of 1889, the great dock strike, and of 1911, the wave of transport strikes of that year. But we have also had to document some very big defeats, in 1892 and 1893, and again in 1912. So, yes, certainly, strikes are part of a strategy which the old unionists, the old craftsmen, frowned on. But they were strikes in season; in other words, there were times when they were wise and successful, and times when those same leaders, Tillett and Mann, famous for their radicalism, were actively discouraging strikes which they predicted would be defeated, and actively promoting peaceful bargaining and the practice of arbitration. In other words, they were concerned to husband their resources and ensure continuity.

The T&G inherited all of that and became in its early years one of the foremost advocates of Joint Industrial Councils, national bargaining, nationally established rates, hours, working conditions. Bevin himself set the pattern at the famous Shaw Inquiry, when he earned the title of 'the dockers' KC' (King's Counsel), the year before the amalgamation.

Let me offer you a checklist of some other questions that we have tried to answer, or at least that we have tried to raise, in our text. We are dealing with a group of industries which were going through a rapid process of technological change. In shipping and the docks and ports, the transition from sail to steam power; in inland transport, the transition from horse-power to the internal combustion engine; the switch from rail to road, a change that begins to appear during our period ...

We have noted the superiority of the general union over the craft unions, which are left standing high and dry as technology by-passes their own specialisms. And we also notice how our unions handled the relationship with different kinds of employers, large international shipping companies, tiny little local carters' organisations, or a brewery company employing a fleet of draymen. We asked the question: why didn't the seamen, the merchant navy members of the NUS, join in the transport amalgamation? Why didn't the railwaymen of the NUR join in? All these are might-have-beens of history, and we have had a look at them.

Why this long Scottish separatism in docks and in road haulage? Why the strong sectionalism and militancy, which was to plague the life of Ernest Bevin, and later of Arthur Deakin, of the London busmen and the London dockers? Why? Indeed, in the case of the London dockers, the problem goes on and on right through the 1950s and '60s, and isn't resolved until the '70s.

What was the role of the Transport Workers' Federation? Why was it so important, and why was Robert Williams' role, which we regard as crucial, buried by subsequent historians? What was Bevin's role in the amalgamation? Was he a bully, or was he a diplomat? What was the effect of the war on state intervention in industrial relations? What relationship has that intervention to the strong identity which the transport workers made with the doctrine of workers' control and industrial democracy? How did the T&G come to have a white-collar Trade Group from the very start in 1922? After all, that was a pretty unusual association of the manual and the non-manual in the early '20s.

Why are the rules the way they are? We have tried to tell the story of Leamington, the first Rules Conference, and to look at the fascinating debates which were held there about structure and constitution. Central power versus devolved power, devolved power to Regions and Trade Groups. Strike ballots, on which there was a fascinating debate: some of the more militant delegates wanted to exclude any rule about strike ballots. Bevin had a persuasive argument for them – you can read all this at length in the text. The selection or election of full-time officers, that debate is there: all the classic debates of trade unionism which have gone on ever since. And finally, what was the role of internationalism and international trade unionism in this formative period?

Reviews

The golden rivet

Royden Harrison

When a London docker reached the bottom of a ship's hold he used to shout: 'I've found the golden rivet' (Ash, p. 50). It is evidently going to be a long rime before we hear that cry from Coates and Topham. Their massive volume must be the longest pre-natal examination in the whole of trade union historiography. After almost 1000 pages the TGWU has only just been born. This is a wonderful, preposterous, brilliant, uneven book which is uncertain about its own identity as well as that of its readers. It seems that there are two more volumes to come. If it is reasonable to require historians of a general union to stick to their last, fairness requires an indication of what that might look like.

Broadly speaking, there are three ways of writing trade union history. There is the straight biographical mode in which the life of an institution is presented in a clear chronological manner. This is not to be despised. It may be more demanding and more rewarding than some pseudo-sociological offering which prides itself upon being more analytic. The late J. B. Williams' masterful *The Derbyshire Miners* or Philip Bagwell's admirable *The Railwaymen* show what can be done in this tradition. Then there is the history which is organised, not around the life story of one institution, but a cluster of occupations. Raymond Postgate pioneered this style of work in his *The Builders' History*. Richard Price returned to the same cluster in *Masters, Unions and Men*. But it was H. A. Turner in his *Trade Union Growth, Structure and Policy*, which was concerned with the cotton unions, who provided one of the most intellectually rigorous of all 'cluster' studies. Finally, trade union history may be written round a place. Sidney Pollard's *History of Labour in Sheffield* is perhaps still the best offering in this genre. A history of a general union needs to take something from all three styles. Hugh Clegg's *General Union: A Study of the National Union of General and Municipal Workers* was predominantly institutional or biographical. Richard Hyman's *The Workers' Union* went for 'cluster' and something more. Coates and Topham are certainly familiar with all these traditions and all these possibilities, but they are unwilling to be constrained within any of them whether they be considered separately or taken together. They do not see themselves as writing a *mere* trade union history. Their concern is with the *Making* and the *Emergence* of the whole Labour Movement. They imagine themselves in a line of descent which runs, not from Williams nor from Postgate nor from Pollard, let alone from Clegg, but from E. P. Thompson's *The Making of the English Working Class*.

Coates and Topham leave this classic work out of their bibliography. However, one senses its influence upon almost every page. It is an ambiguous legacy because it can mislead as well as inspire. The expropriation of bits of Thompson's vocabulary is quite allowable. In fact it makes more sense to relate 'Making' to the history of an institution than to the history of a class or social formation. But the nature of their subject makes it undesirable that they should follow Thompson in his preoccupation with the English to the exclusion of the Scots and the Welsh. (As ports and places, Glasgow and Cardiff mattered more than Hull between 1870 and 1922, Dyos and Aldcroft, 1969, p. 247 et seq.) Again, one must be on guard against the wonderful artistic power of Thompson's book. It tends to sweep the reader away so that s/he hardly dare pause for thought or ask: is that true? If s/he does stop and ask that question s/he may find occasion to answer: well, not entirely! A more serious danger in treating Thompson as the Master is that one fails to master his method. Many of his admirers fail to recognise that along with the art there is associated a high level of intellectual engagement. Below the apparently free play of the scholarly imagination there lies a sequence of well-structured questions: questions whose imperatives control the whole literary enterprise. In fact, it is exactly this quality which raises Thompson above his distinguished predecessors, J. L. and Barbara Hammond. Coates and Topham do understand this. At some cost to their own stylistic accomplishment, they have brought the controlling questions into the open and even broken off their narrative in order to address them directly. Thus, the first part of this first volume is ruled by a concern with the New Unionism. What was it? When was it? How was it that it was when it was rather than earlier or later?

The authors maintain that all modern historians understand by the New Unionism:

1. The organisation of workers deemed to be 'unskilled'.
2. The recruitment of members from a wide range of industries and occupations, which is to say that, commonly although not always, they were open, general unions.
3. The commitment to be 'fighting unions', charging low

subscriptions, avoiding heavy friendly-society benefits, and using their funds primarily for strike pay.
4. Militancy.
5. Political radicalism, often embracing socialism and questioning the older unions' adherence to the Liberal Party.
To these five generally accepted qualities we would add:
6. They made space for the organisation of women, and indeed the whole movement drew an example from the matchgirls' strike ... (Coates and Topham, 1991, p 96).

Critics might complain that point 4 adds little or nothing to 3. More interestingly, they might suggest that the New Unionism always requires an 'explosion' not only in trade union membership, but in Labour papers and periodicals. Still more importantly, it relates to changes in the organisation of well-established unions, such as engineers or coal-miners. This is associated with the undeniable fact that a contingent of members recruited from well-established industries and trades, miners or engineers, are needed to abandon their labour aristocratic traditions and identify themselves with the cause of the plebeians.

However, the problem is very much more about when than about what. Everyone would agree that the attempts at General Unionism made in the 1830s do not count. Of course, there was an explosive growth in membership. To be sure, the organisers and agitators cursed 'the pukes and exclusives', called themselves socialists, and looked forward to the millennium. But One Big Union in the shape of the Grand National Consolidated belonged to another world of labour: one which did not last and which was remote from developments after 1850 (Cole, 1953). Perhaps Coates and Topham devote too much attention to this matter. They are certainly correct to follow the Webbs in noting how Robert Owen despised and rejected political action while the New Unionists, properly so-called, attached the highest importance to it (Webb and Webb, 1893, p. 404).

The serious discussion relates to the question of whether the New Unionism started in the 1870s or in the late eighties/early nineties or whether it can be said to have established any serious presence before the years immediately preceding the Great War. Coates and Topham are far from neglecting the mid-Victorian experience, but they do not wonder about it quite enough. In the early 1870s all the components of the New Unionism were present: there was the revolt of the field; the uprising in the mines; the revolt within the old unions like the engineers in favour of the 9-hour day; the assumption of a leading position by the gas workers; dockers coming out on strike for the tanner; the advent of the first syndicated workers' papers, the *Examiner* group (Jones, 1982, pp. 297-316); help and encouragement from near-Marxists like Patrick Hennessey and Charles Keen. The Labour Protection League grew in 6 months from a membership of 1,200 to one of 30,000. It went out beyond the docks and organised engineers' labourers in Milwall and formed branches among dustmen, slopmen and scavengers. At the very least, this was a brilliant anticipation of almost everything which was to follow. Why then did it not stick? Why, with the exception of a vestigial form of the Labour Protection League, was it all consigned to oblivion while Burns, Mann, Tillett, Annie Besant, Bernard Shaw and the *Star* – never mind Cardinal Manning – were to be enshrined for ever in the heart of labour historiography and, indeed, the popular memory? It is not because Marx had more influence dead than alive – although he may have had. Rather it must be understood in terms of profound economic, social and legal changes which together gave a new possibility to trade unionism. The grand fact is that the volume of shipping requiring harbour services rose five-fold between 1870 and 1914. The demand for dock labour, the different orders of dock labour and the real rewards which those labourers received were profoundly affected by refrigeration. To be sure, the cool storage of beef was carried out from the USA to England in 1870, but it was carried out in ships' holds by means of ice-salt mixtures and it was not very successful. It was only after 1880 that whole carcasses of frozen mutton and quantities of beef were shipped in vastly increasing amounts from Australasia in refrigerated ships at temperatures at which quality was hardly affected (Critchell and Raymond, 1912). Between 1870 and 1896 the meat consumption per head of the British people went up by almost one-third, but the proportion of imported meat trebled. Soon 40% of the meat consumed in Britain came from overseas. The preservation of fruits in a frozen state occurred rather later and with less dramatic effects. The importance of refrigeration is commonplace among economic historians (Hobsbawm, 1969, p. 162), but here its effects should have been considered in relation to coastal and oceanic shipping. The impact upon the sorts of dock labour required should have been taken into account. These developments were important for the standard of life of the unskilled, dockers and non-dockers alike. In short, to understand why the New Unionism had a more lasting impact around 1890 than it had 20 years earlier one must attend to the way in which the altered conditions of supply and demand for dock labour emerged. If, as the Webbs stipulated: 'A trade union ... is a continuous association of wage-earners for the purpose of maintaining or improving the conditions of their employment' (1893, p. 1), it is necessary that supply and demand have already conspired to lift the real wages of the labourers above the margin of subsistence. An inadequate appreciation of this makes it impossible to answer the question: why 1890 and not 1870?

Coates and Topham also underrate the importance of changes in the law relating to trade unions. These made it much harder to take off in 1870 than was the case 20 years later. Thus, the gas workers were always in the van of the New Unionism. But this led them behind bars in 1870, whereas they became the heroes of the hour at their second attempt (Webb and Webb, 1893, pp. 268-269). Characteristically, Gladstone associated his Trade Union Act of 1871 (which conferred great immunities) with his Criminal Law Amendment Act, which criminalised peaceful picketing. The social content of all this was that the closed unions of the labour aristocrats were secured while their members subjected their employers to unilateral regulation. The plebeians in the new industrial or general unions, who had to have recourse to mass strikes, were likely to fall foul of the law. This situation where there was one legal status for the top strata and another for the lower was ended by an ill-judged prosecution of some London cabinet makers (*ibid.*, p. 274). Their imprisonment and the campaign which culminated in their release made it clear that a further reform of the law was essential. But by that time the 'Great Depression' had begun and the New Unionism had lost its opportunity.

Coates and Topham leave the impression that they have not mastered these complexities. Thus, they seem to be over-impressed by the fearsome rhetoric of Disraeli's subsequent Conspiracy and Protection of Property Act, 1875. Like the ill-advised magistrate in Chesterfield who punished many men for 'watching and besetting' during the 1984-1985 strike, they made, at best, a highly selective reading of the Act. In fact, just as section 3 of that measure begins by limiting the nature of an indictable conspiracy, so section 7 ends by curtailing the scope of watching and besetting. It lays it down that: attending at or near the house or place where a person resides, or works, or carries on business, or happens to be, or the approach to such a house or place, in order merely to obtain or communicate information, shall not be deemed a watching or besetting within the meaning of this section.[1] Mr Disraeli had to explain to the Queen that all this was not designed to criminalise the organised working class but rather 'to soften the feelings of the multitude' (Letter, 29 June 1875).[2] This it did, but too late to help the precocious New Unionists of the early 1870s. In any event it was the inadequate and irregular earnings of the unskilled, even more than the savagery of the law, which put paid to the efforts of agricultural labourers, dockers and gas workers.

One is left with a strong sense that Coates and Topham would have been well-advised to reduce an over-long book by sharply diminishing the 100 pages or so that they devote to mid-Victorian labour. They are not at home here as they are when they come to discuss subsequent periods. Their scholarly apparatus collapses. They support assertions about basic economic data by a reference to a high authority, but not to his nor anyone else's published work (Coates and Topham, p. 120n). They make George Odger blow hot and cold concerning Ben Tilletts' Tea Operatives and General Labourers' Union ten years after that great, radical shoemaker was dead![3]

The problem of how best to think about the problem of the New Unionism recurs when we reflect about what happened after 1889 as well as what happened before it. The authors are tempted to cast Hugh Clegg and his associates as adversaries when it comes to this matter. They complain – and it is a very plausible complaint – that Clegg imagined that the New Unionism narrowly averted a cot death in 1889-1890. He did, indeed, suggest that the new unions were eased out in 12 months, with scarcely a ripple of public interest (Clegg et al., 1964). They rightly go to great lengths to dispute this conclusion.

Having chronicled, once again, how the New Unionism arrived through the epic struggle of the match girls, gas workers and dockers, they then devote 200 pages to what they term Defeat, Defence and Defiance. This is followed by an examination of the long years of 'Hanging on' and the transition from 1900-1910. They concluded with an account of 1911 seen as the year of the 'Big Bang' in which the New Unions were not born, but attained some maturity. They correctly insist that the falling away of the New Unions' membership between 1890 and 1896 does not amount to their annihilation. It was a severe and prolonged setback which can be explained by the trade cycle; changes in the technology and structure of transport; and, not least, more effective anti-labour policies by the employers and the State. 'In all ports, regardless of their peculiarities, the combination of trade cycle downswing and competitive pressures ensured that the employers' tolerance of the new unions would be shortlived. The force of the new unionism was to be confronted by the counterforce of a fighting, militant, anti-union employers' organisation: the Shipping Federation, formed just after the 1889 strike' (Coates and Topham, p. 131). This whole passage of argument appears to be well supported. The men and institutions that came into prominence around 1890 held their ground in a way that the generation of 1870 did not. The exception would be the Labour Protection League, but although this survived throughout the entire period it became a small and relatively unimportant union. However, it would be unwise to imagine that Clegg and his colleagues have been effectively revised right across the board. There is really much less at issue between Coates and Topham on the one hand and Clegg, Fox and Thompson on the other than a hasty reader might imagine. Thus, when it comes to the role of the Socialists (particularly those of them raised within the trade union movement itself) or the way in which the General Unions relied upon a relatively hard industrial core, there is little or nothing dividing the two teams. The contrast has more to do with matters of style than of substance. Clegg has a strong distaste for what he regards as enthusiasm or romanticism. He is always happier in denial than he is in affirmation. Coates and Topham are men of a very different temper. There is little more to it than that.[4]

Since Coates and Topham have been distinguished exponents of Workers' Control in both theory and practice, it was only to be expected that they would supply a sympathetic, as well as an informed and highly readable, account of Syndicalism and the Great Unrest of 1911-1914 (see Coates and Topham, 1968). They acknowledge their enjoyment of Dangerfield's brilliant work (Dangerfield, 1936), but they are too canny to follow his conjectures about the psychology or the metaphysics of violence. They are more interested in the evidence relating to falling real wages, although they treat it with great caution, preferring to stress the growth of relative deprivation. Few historians would question the reality of relative deprivation, whether considered objectively or subjectively, nor would they doubt its importance, if not necessarily its centrality, when it comes to explaining the pre-war explosion. Sydicalists, particularly French ones, affected to scorn Recognition. Why bargain when One Big Union, strong in mind and body, could abolish the entire Boss Class by Direct Action? Coates and Topham are far too shrewd to miss the weakness which often lurked behind this bravado. Those who could not bring management to the negotiating table assured everyone that only cowards and failures aspired to do so.

As they point out, the outbreak of war soon exposed many a militant pretension for what it was. The coming of full employment ensured that the employers and the State would welcome a negotiated peace with Labour even if they still sought an unconditional surrender from the Germans. Such a peace implied the need for Recognition. The authors are at their very best when they discuss Recognition; its meaning and its ramifications (see pp. 71-73). They are less consistent and less persuasive when they turn to the law relating to trade unions.

The second part of this first volume may be read as an account of why some unions did, and other unions did not, seek closer unity. Broadly speaking, those sections of uniformed working class which enjoyed a reasonable prospect of industrial unionism such as the railwaymen and the merchant seamen, were less interested in a wider unity than others, also employed in and around harbours, where the core group was less and less self-conscious. By 1914 the railwaymen were still divided, but they had survived everything which the Courts could do to them. As for the sailors, perhaps the problem was, as Harry Bridges expressed it: 'Sailors is bums!'[5] Coates and Topham do not have such a quick way with the problem as Bridges. On the contrary, they point to the positive, formative influence exercised by the seamen during the earlier stages of development of the New Unionism (1991, p. 88). It was quite late in the day before the sailors abandoned militancy and became identified with what is now referred to as the 'New Realism': single union no strike agreements. Plainly the problem of general unionism is located in a middle along that continuum that relates the successful closed, craft union at one end to the flotsam and jetsam, the residuum, of unorganisable underclass labourers to be found at the other. Why should the successful craft union which is able to limit the supply of labour by restricting the number of apprentices, the length of working hours and the size of the task, etc. join a federation, never mind an industrial or a general union? How can the unorganised ever be persuaded that they are anything but unorganisable? How can those located between these two extremes be induced to believe that an amalgamation proposal will bring them more new members than it costs them, involve them in more beneficial disputes than sacrificial ones, diminish their bureaucratic burdens rather than increase them, and facilitate 'asset stripping' rather than expose them to it? What orders of temptation will be necessary before incumbent officials will be ready to sacrifice their appointments in the interests of wider unity? G. D. H. Cole and others who identified the claims of Reason and Humanity imagined that General Unions should serve as clearing houses, locations within which the hitherto unorganised might be prepared for those industrial unions into which they should hive off (Cole and Mellor, 1913). The cure for such heroic, rational delusions is a close study of the concluding chapters of this work. They should be made obligatory reading for all teachers and students of Industrial Relations and Economics. Coates and Topham remind us that there are times when dreary evidence of historians becomes more compelling than the assumptions of economists or the dreadful cautions of political scientists. Of course, they also remind us that hope and success are still possible.

The authors of this History are at their best when they recover the personalities of the men who led the way to Amalgamation in 1922: Harry Gosling, Robert Williams, and, above all, Ernie Bevin. In the case of Gosling this is not too difficult since he supplied one of the most charming and informative of all proletarian autobiographies (Gosling, 1927). Bob Williams is quite another matter because this brilliant and courageous fighter has been relegated into the rank of a non-person by the Communist Party and its apologists. Making excellent use of the little known Transport Workers' Federation newsletter, the *Weekly Record,* which was edited by Williams, they recover this extraordinary personality and do justice to his great achievement. In any case, it would have been hard to rescue Williams from beneath the vast, protective shade of Ernest Bevin. Despite the presence of an authoritative 'Life' (Bullock, 1966), we are provided with a fresh and convincing portrait of the Big Man who did more than anyone else to make 'One Big Union'. His emergence as 'the Dockers' Q.C.' in the famous Shaw Inquiry makes one of the most compelling and important chapters in the entire book.

In general, it would be hard to over-praise the thumb-nail sketches of the Transport Workers' leaders which are to be found in this volume. The portraits are both accurate and drawn with deep feeling. This applies to the men and women whom one senses enjoy the authors' support as well as to those who arouse their antipathy. Whether it is Labour's Lost Leader, John Burns; the charismatic Tom Mann; the gifted but wayward Ben Tillett; the able, but eminently careerist, James Sexton; the perceptive, self-styled prophet of 'free Labour', William Collison; the outstanding organiser of the Sailor and Firemen's Union, Havelock Wilson; or the magnificent stormy petrel James Larkin, the hero of the Dublin lock-out of 1913 – justice is done to them all.

Of course this does not mean that all that needs to be said about them has been said. Coates and Topham have whetted the reader's appetite for more about Robert Williams. As for Tom Mann, it is fortunate that the publication of their work has coincided with the appearance of a full-scale study by Professor Chuschichi Tsuzuki ...

Bibliography

Ash, T. no date. *Childhood Days: The Docks and Dock Slang*, London, privately published

Bagwell, P. 1963. *The Railwaymen*, London, Allen and Unwin.

Bullock, A. 1960. *The Life and Times of Ernest Bevin, Vol. 1 Trade Union Leader*, London, Heinemann

Clegg, H. A., Fox, A. and Thompson, A. F. 1964. *A History of British Trade Unions since 1889, Vol. 1, 1889-1910*, Oxford, OUP

Clegg, H. 1954. *General Union: A Study of the National Union of General and Municipal Workers*, Oxford, Blackwell

Coates, K. and Topham, A. 1968. *Industrial Democracy in Great Britain: A Book of Readings and Witnesses for Workers' Control,* Oxford, Blackwell

Coates, K. and Topham, T. 1991. *The History of the Transport and General Workers' Union. Vol. 1, Parts 1 and 2, The Making of the Transport and General Workers' Union: The Emergence of the Labour Movement 1870-1922*, Oxford, Blackwell

Cole, G. D. H. 1953. *Attempts at General Union,* London, Macmillan

Cole, G. D. H. and Mellor, W. 1913. *The Greater Unionism*, London, National Labour Press

Critchell, J. and Raymond, J. 1912. *A History of the Frozen Meat Trade*, London, Constable

Dangerfield, G. 1936. *The Strange Death of Liberal England*, London, Constable

Dyos, H. J. and Aldcroft, D. H. 1969. *British Transport*, Leicester, Leicester University Press

Gosling, H. 1927. *Up and Down Stream,* London, Methuen

Hammond, J. L. and Hammond, B. 1911. *The Village Labourer*, London, Longmans

Hammond, J. L. and Hammond, B. 1917. *The Town Labourer*, London, Longmans

Hammond, J. L. and Hammond, B. 1920. *The Skilled Labourer*, London, Longmans

Harrison, R. 1965. *Before the Socialists*, London, Routledge

Hobsbawm, E. J. 1969. *Industry and Empire,* London, Weidenfeld

Hyman, R. 1971. *The Workers' Union,* Oxford, OUP

Jones, A. 1982. Workmen's advocates: ideology and class in a mid-Victorian newspaper, in Shattock, J. and Wolff, M. (eds), *The Victorian Periodical Press,* Leicester, Leicester University Press

Moneypenny, W. F. and Buckle, G. E. 1910-1920. *The Life of Benjamin Disraeli: Earl of Beaconsfield* (6 Vols), London, John Murray

Phillips, G. and Whitside, N. 1985. *Casual Labour: The Unemployment Question in the Port Transport Industry, 1880-1970*, Oxford, OUP

Pollard, S. 1959. *History of Labour in Sheffield,* Liverpool, Liverpool University Press

Postgate, R. 1923. *The Builders' History*, London, National Federation of Building Trade Operatives

Price, R. 1980. *Masters, Unions and Men*, Cambridge, CUP

Spain, J. 1991. Trade Unionists, Gladstonian liberals and the Labout Law, in Biagini, E. and Reid, A. (eds) *Currents of Radicalism*, Cambridge, CUP

Thompson, E. P. 1963. *The Making of the English Working Class*, London, Gollancz

Tsuzuki, C. 1991. *Tom Mann 1856-1941: The Challenges of Labour*, Oxford, OUP

Turner, H. A. 1962. *Trade Union Growth, Structure and Policy*, London, Allen & Unwin

Webb, S. and Webb, B. 1894. *History of Trade Unionism*, London, Longmans

Williams, J. E. 1962. *The Derbyshire Miners*, London, Allen & Unwin

Notes

1. 38 & 39 Vict. c 86, final lines in section 7.
2. For a somewhat different way of interpreting these matters, see Spain, 1991, pp. 109-133.
3. The funeral of George Odger, *Weekly Despatch*, 11 and 18 March, 1877
4. Compare Clegg, Fox and Thompson, 1964, pp. 87-96 with the attack mounted by Coates and Topham, 1991, p. 115 et seq., pp. 281-282 and p. 394
5. Harry Bridges to the reviewer at the University of Wisconsin, Madison, winter 1964-1965.
6. Phillips and Whitside (1985) is invaluable but it hardly addresses this problem. Dr David England of the Open University has been using the material in the Charles Booth Collection in the London School of Economics. We may expect something important from him in the near future.

Cambridge Journal of Economics, 1992

In reply

Excerpts from Tony Topham's letter to Ken Coates, dated 21 January 1993, responding to some points in Royden Harrison's review.

... You are correct in recalling the source of our information about Tillett receiving advice from George Odger; it was himself. I enclose the pages – Ben refers to Odger not once, but twice. I have also verified, from other sources, that Odger did indeed die in 1877! ...

On refrigeration, I have nothing useful to add ... I imagine that humping frozen carcasses of Australasian mutton and beef (not Argentinian?) was just another manual task – out of ship's hold in slings, on to rail, or river craft, or lorry. I just don't know the answers, except that obviously it was a welcome new, and substantial, trade for both employers and dockers. *Was* it less perishable, as you suppose, once it had arrived in port? Was refrigeration installed also in quayside warehouses? (It occurs that it must have had a lot to do with advancing labour demand inshore, at the big meat markets.) I shall see Walt this evening, and probe his intelligence and expertise on this technical – possibly substantive – question ...

[Royden's] second paragraph amounts to a complaint that we don't fit into any model precedent of trade union histories. To which the answer, ('Why should it, when our subject is as big as the TGWU became?') does not depend upon reference to E.P. Thompson's work. Why should we have included him in the bibliography? His book doesn't extend beyond the 1830s. But Royden then goes on to make the quite erroneous point about following EPT into a preoccupation with the English. To assert that we exclude the Scots and the Welsh (he doesn't mention the Irish!) is just wrong ...

Cardiff, specified by Royden, gets as much attention as Hull, and Glasgow is fully integrated, too, especially as a prime example of separatism amongst its dockers. And it is NOT parochial to contest Royden's relegation of Hull. In 1893 its experience was crucial. It was generally referred to as 'the third port', and I think that a count of the number of conferences of national labour movement organisations held in Hull in our period, compared with Cardiff and Glasgow, would indicate its relative importance for trade unionism. Moreover, it commands attention for its very large role in the Free Labour Movement ...

'My best read'

Jack Jones

The Making of the Transport and General Workers' Union is a splendid addition to the literature on trade union and industrial history. It is subtitled *The Emergence of the Labour Movement 1870-1922* and it was my best read this year because of the clarity and liveliness of the writing. History which I thought I knew pretty well was given a new punch, which greatly encourages an old hand like me to still preach the trade union message. The book should be read by all who wish to see a revitalised trade union and labour movement. History written in the inimitable style of Coates and Topham has much to teach us.

Morning Star, 30 December 1991

'Vivid pictures'

Julie Lindsay

... I was surprised that a full account of the union's history had not been written before. In this one the authors go into minute detail, but in each section the events are presented in a style that makes interestingly light reading. The reader does not become bombarded with facts and figures. Both volumes highlight the hard times and problems encountered before the amalgamation, giving vivid pictures of the characters involved. Ernest Bevin in particular played an enormous role and won the hearts of many.

Whether you're a student of industrial relations or simply interested in trade union history, the work is worth the reading. Don't be intimidated by the size or length of the book, I found it very easy to read.

Landworker, August/September 1991

Vital issue of recognition

Jim Mortimer

Ken Coates and Tony Topham have written a superb first volume of the history of the Transport and General Workers' Union ...This book is very readable. The history never becomes boring. It is fast moving and the language is plain and straightforward. In other words, the book is well written.

The history of the formative years is not one of successive victories. Far from it. There are as many defeats as triumphs. Yet, it is precisely this realty that provides the inspiration. Defeat does not lead to trade union extinction. The unions survive, though often in a very weakened form, but they rise again in greater strength. The struggle of workers never ceases.

Many active trade unionists are aware, for example, of the historic significance of the 1889 dock strike. How many, on the other hand, are aware of the many years of effort that preceded it, or the many difficult years and defeats that followed? By 1895 the employers had conducted a largely successful counter-offensive and trade union membership was much reduced. By 1910 a new mood was emerging. It was followed by the years of the great unrest immediately before the First World War. The dockworkers were among many whose vigour and militancy reached unprecedented levels.

Giant personalities of the trade union movement stride through the pages of these two books. In the first the commanding figure is Tom Mann, followed closely but the more erratic Ben Tillett. Both are described sympathetically. Their contribution was enormous. In the second book two leaders come to the front, above all Robert Williams and Ernest Bevin. There are also glimpses of Larkin and Connolly.

Robert Williams became the secretary of the National Transport Workers' Federation. The authors describe him as a leader of outstanding merit. His administrative abilities were probably unmatched among his colleagues and he was very hard-working. He was sensitive to the differences between the affiliated organisations, and he was a strong socialist, but his militancy never ran away from his understanding of what was possible in given circumstances.

Ernest Bevin, more than anybody else, was the architect of the TGWU. He had a vision which has stood the test of time. He saw the need for solidarity, amalgamation, discipline and effective administrative control, but he also recognised that trade union groups should enjoy a measure of autonomy to be responsive to their members.

Bevin, certainly in these early years, was no right-winger. His opinions, unlike those of James Sexton, the Liverpool dockers' leader, were on the left rather than on the right of the movement. He never lost sight of his main aim: to build a strong amalgamated union based upon the occupational interests of the membership. He also always attached an importance to an independent labour press.

One vital issue, running like a thread through the history of these formative years, was the importance of trade union recognition. The task was to maintain the presence of trade unionism even in the most adverse circumstances. Bevin seized the opportunity to develop the scope of collective bargaining. His role before the Shaw Inquiry into dockers' conditions, and his influence in making the flour-milling Joint Industrial Council a model for so many others, demonstrated his capacity.

This book has been written by authors with a strong socialist commitment. Hence, they write with understanding of the motivation of many of the pioneers of the TGWU ... It is this socialist commitment, combined with a scholarly and objective study of the history of trade unionism, which enables them to focus attention on a recurring and sometimes contradictory aspect of the struggle. Trade unionism represents a challenge to any unilateral control exercised by employers. When this is achieved, the union becomes part of the regulatory employment mechanism within the existing social system ...

Socialist Campaign Group News, July 1991

'Wonderfully strong on people'

Diana Warwick

I cannot remember when I enjoyed social (or socialist) history so much. I liked particularly the bullishness of the two authors who are compelled by a notion of internationalist democracy as the hope of working people, but who write with the conviction that 'history must not be written with bias, both sides should be given, even if there is only one side'.

This is the 'pre-history' of the Transport and General Workers' Union (TGWU) – the book ends at 1922, usually regarded by trade unions as the birth day of the TGWU ... It is, in addition, a fascinating account of the influences on the early growth of the Labour Party in localities like Hull, Liverpool, Bradford and Bristol. It is a big story and this is a big book, of over 1,000 pages, which never becomes tedious.

It is a sweet coincidence that the publication of this dramatic history coincides with the election of the TGWU's Bill Morris as Britain's first black trade union general secretary. Bill Morris heralded his election by declaring that he would re-unite the union. This book chronicles the long and fraught process which (over 50 years) enabled Ernest Bevin, in 1922, to unite a huge range of craft and general unions into One Big Union.

The authors reach back a long way to try to establish an umbilical link between present industrial problems and the 1870s. A recurring and relevant theme is the unerring way in which it is always during an upturn in the economy that labour can 'answer back'. The industrial fortunes of workers like stevedores, mechanics and lightermen wax and wane through this book along with economic booms and recessions. The old sectionalism of the fragmented 19th century trade unions reasserted itself in each depression after a boom, despite the efforts of the One Big Unionists. The authors chart the disaffection and disarray which plagued the notion of a general union for generations.

There are some wonderful vignettes – like the Byrant and May match girls, historically sanctified – whose final straw was not, apparently, appalling health hazards but a docking of pay to build a statue of Gladstone in the factory forecourt.

Some themes don't change. I choose three among many, which seem to show how the present is yoked to the past. First 'claimed' membership as against 'actual' membership was as much an area of contention for the Labour Representation Committee in 1900 as it is for the TUC now.

Second, there was a suspicion of the pragmatism of the clever young men of the International Labour Party (ILP), 'better heeled and less turbulent than their founding fathers, courting new allies'; the current TGWU General Secretary Ron Todd seems to express similar caution about the 'new realists' in his frank and moving foreword. Third, 100 years ago Labour representatives in the new political party did not want to be bound to any overall political philosophy: and disputes about who calls the tune in the Labour Party have gone on ever since.

This book is wonderfully strong on people. They burst with larger-than-life characters. Nineteenth-century socialists are vividly and sometimes eccentrically recreated. Tillett, a leading labour figure, wrestles with the problems of creating a colossal picketing system using advice from a lecture by the future Archbishop of Canterbury on the Strategy and Tactics of Napoleon. Tom Mann, self-educated craft unionist, who inspired the disputes of the eighties and nineties, countered the sops of bread, circuses and old-aged pensions with a 'literate and powerful democracy'. There is even a well-attested villain, Collison, who has a poignant meeting with Eleanor Marx while he fingers a ship's rivet hurled at him by an angry picket.

Throughout, awareness of class drives activists on. I'm reminded of H. B. Davis's comment that 'class-conscious leaders make the best organisers. They are harder to bluff, harder to bribe and harder to fool'.

Details sparkle. The style is trenchant and every character is vividly drawn. The research is painstaking. There is much previously unexplored material. There is imaginative use of transcripts from official enquiries and public meetings, as well as the huge TGWU archive, to help the 'plot' hang together.

Descriptions of ordinary people's lives at the turn of the century are harrowing. Humour is personalised: workers call their foreman 'Rembrandt' when he says 'let me put you in the picture' and it's Sheriff who asks 'where's the hold-up lads, where's the hold-up?'

This narrative is a lively and invigorating read for those who want to know why passionate men and women band together through unspeakable hardship in order to forge their vision of a secure future of equal opportunity for all working people. Irrepressibly and vividly, the authors convey what Sir Bill MacCarthy has called 'the organised power of ordinary men and women'. They reinforce the imperatives (and the vision) which have sustained union activists and officials over the last 100 years.

This work is a must for any student of industrial relations. The layout of the book, – with short snappy sections and headings which guide the reader through a wealth of material – make them accessible to the general or grasshopper reader.

The Guardian, 11 July 1991

'Breathlessly exciting from first to last'

Kenneth O. Morgan

For British trade unions (to quote Neil Kinnock's verdict on Arthur Scargill) the Thatcher experience was 'another Gallipoli'. For decades after 1945, they were clients of what many regarded as the post-war consensus. Whether as agents of corporatism, with bosses like Deakin or Gormley, or prophets of industrial revolt like Cousins or Scargill, the unions were pivotal to British politics. But, since 1979, these pretensions have been shattered.

The 1980s saw a series of retreats; partly, of course, as the result of Thatcherism's ideological animus, but also of appalling miscalculations by union leaders from the 'winter of discontent' in

1979 to the catastrophic failure of the miners' strike. The unions have lost clout and charisma. In 1987, they played a smaller part in Labour's electoral campaign than at any time since 1906. Yet, for all their diminished influence, they remain central to the prospects of any future Labour government ...

... The contrast between the uncertainties of the present and the heroic achievement of historic struggles is admirably brought out in Coates and Topham's magisterial study of the origins of the TGWU from the dockers' struggles in the 1880s to the amalgamation under Ernest Bevin's leadership in 1922. This mammoth work is breathlessly exciting from first to last; not one of its thousand pages is wasted. We read of mighty conflicts – the 1889 dock strike, Labour's *annus mirabilis* of 1911, the titanic confrontations with Lloyd George after the war – and a succession of dynamic leaders: Mann, Tillett, Sexton, Bevin, and that brilliant meteor Bob Williams. There are also *leitmotivs* of many central features in trade union history: the quest for 'one big union', pressure for local industrial democracy or forms of syndicalism, a genuine internationalism almost unique in the British labour world.

As a story of industrial struggle, the logic of this history is clear-cut. What is more ambiguous is the contribution of the TGWU to Labour politics. Although described by Lord McCarthy as 'the Godfather of the Labour Party', the TGWU has offered an uncertain approach to parliamentary action. Bevin himself felt that it was in the industrial arena that the class struggle would truly be waged. The Transport Workers have mirrored the political traumas of the unions as a whole. Intimacy with Labour governments contrasts with the indirection that had such dire results in the late 1970s, especially under the wholly disastrous regime of Moss Evans.

In recent times, the TGWU has been politically sidelined. Neil Kinnock showed the world that he could do without its block vote in dispensing with unilateralism. More than most unions, the TGWU is caught in a time-warp. It has been less effective in Labour's policy review exercises than, say, the AUEW, NUPE or many white-collar unions.

If, under the heartening leadership of Britain's first black general secretary, Bill Morris, the union can find a more creative and contemporary role within the political culture of the left, then the next Labour government will surely benefit. Then the Godfather could abandon the Honoured Society and tread what Bob Williams called 'the path to power'.

New Statesman

'... *the special merit lies in being within the spirit of unionism* ...'

Eric Hobsbawm

Trade unions have long since learned to let scholars write their histories, but the danger of academic labour history is that it tends to look past the non-academic reader. Both the T&G and the authors are to be congratulated for keeping the ordinary reader in mind. Not that many members of the union are likely to curl up with the first two of a series of volumes which, by page 909, have just about seen the union through its birth, even though there is plenty of drama in the years from 1870 to 1922 which they cover. The great struggles of those years can bear retelling – the 1889 London Dock Strike, the 1890s lock-outs, the Belfast battles of 1907, the Dublin war of 1913, the labour explosions of 1911, the drama of the 1912 London defeat, Ernest Bevin's dramatic confrontation with the statisticians of the Shaw Inquiry. The great, sometimes over-life-size personalities of those days – Burns, Mann, Tillett, Sexton, and not least Bevin himself, not forgetting Jim Larkin and Connolly – remain irresistible, and Coates and Topham pay proper attention to these sometimes (but not always) overdeveloped egos, though one suspects that their heart is less with the great public orators than with quieter men, like Harry Gosling, the first president of the T&G, and Robert Williams of the National Transport Workers' Federation. Indeed, if Coates and Topham have a real hero, it is this coal-trimmer from a small Welsh union, whom they set out to rehabilitate.

Nevertheless, the special merit of this book lies in being written, not merely about a union, but in the spirit of unionism and the men – at this stage there were no women – who constructed this union. It can no longer be taken for granted that this is automatically understood in the 1990s, perhaps not even by all unionists.

The fundamental problem of the history of the T&G is that of British union history as a whole. Why did it develop its characteristic pattern of nation-wide catch-all 'general unions'? The more specific problem is the largest of these 'general unions' in Britain developed around the waterside workers, and why, in spite of systematic attempts at general amalgamation, which both sides favoured in principle, in the end the two general unions of the 'New Unionism' of

1889, the London dockers and the London gas-workers' unions, failed to fuse between 1914 and 1922, thus creating the two rival giants we know. Coates and Topham are keenly aware of these questions.

The first question raises the issue of 'industrial unionism', much debated between 1910 and 1922, which the authors dismiss a little too easily. For a while it is true that many of the proposals to rationalise British union structure on industrial lines came from '"social engineers" of both left-wing and (later) right-wing persuasion' (p. 562) with *a priori* definitions of what constituted an 'industry', or was copied from German trade union structure, in fact the core of the T&G was industrial rather than general, namely transport. Indeed, the reason why the two great general unions of 1889 in the end remained separate was, as the authors recognise, that only one of them was really general in its aspirations, dreaming of the ideal of 'one man, one card' which would allow him to take jobs everywhere. In fact, most of its own membership did not consist of free-flowing 'general' labour, but of protected, or at any rate defensible enclaves, but this was an unintended by-product of their evolution. They were not faced by the constant dilemma that confronted the port-and-road-transport unions, namely how, on the one hand, to recruit a volatile casual labour force in occupations easily entered and with fluctuating demand, while, on the other hand, protecting their territories, once organised, against an influx of labour. The general workers' unions and the transport workers thus had different approaches to organisation, which, in spite of their common interest in a merger, were recognised as incompatible even before 1914, as is well brought out in the chapter on the debates of 1913-14.

That the T&G emerged, not out of a comprehensive but a truncated unionisation of transport workers, is not surprising, and well explained. Railway workers, whose status was quite different, even when they provided the dock labour force, (pp.629-30), never affiliated to the National Transport Workers' Federation. The Sailors, who did, have traditionally – and necessarily – been closely geared to port unionism, but the nature of their occupation brought them only into intermittent contact with land, and they lacked the rooted waterside communities which the authors understand so well (pp. 450, 461-63). From a close initial symbiosis the two kinds of union were to diverge, and not only in Britain. (This reviewer remembers being told by the late Harry Bridges of the International

Longshoremen and Warehouse Men, with some conviction: 'All seamen are bums.') What was left to organise centred on docks and horses which linked the waterside transport to land transport, the carters easily mutating into the tramway, bus, lorry and general motor vehicle drivers. It should be noticed, however, that the largest inland transport unions did not join until 1916-18. The core of the future T&G was dock labour and dockside transport, Bevin's Bristol, were one union organised both dockers and carters with departmental autonomy for each, providing the model for its future structure.

Yet the T&G could not, for historic reasons, have developed as a pure transport industry union, even though the National Transport Workers' Federation, whose role in its genesis the authors rightly stress, refused the affiliation of non-transport workers, and even though the original T&G did not include, or intend including, the Workers' Union, which was eventually to give it its major industrial and Midlands bases. (Had that union merged after World War I with the Municipal Employees and the National Amalgamated Union of Labour, as was planned, it would have become part of the GMBTU and the history of Bevin's union would have been very different, but the reasons for this failure, more ideological than structural, do not belong in Coates and Topham's book.) The Dockers' Union was not a pure transport union. Indeed, it had survived as a union only because it had extended into other industries. As Bevin put it in 1917 in what is rightly described as a 'cool and prescient speech': 'Industrial Unionism was alright in theory. Necessity is driving us to amalgamation, but not in (this) form' (P. 635).

The chief interest of this history, or at least this instalment of it, lies in the light it throws on the strategies and structural logic of the attempts to rationalise trade union patterns in absence of any authority capable of imposing any single national pattern. For obvious reasons the problems are seen from a union point of view, though the point of view of the state, as represented by the great civil service creators of the industrial relations system, is well recognised. Perhaps the point of view of the employers, bigoted and obstinate as they often were, is sometimes neglected. The dramatic fall in productivity and discipline which followed successful labour triumphs on the waterside (as Lovell showed) is underplayed.

However, not the least of the merits of this impressive work is that the authors show a real understanding even of those with whom labour historians have rarely empathised – men like 'Free Labour'

Collison and 'Osborne Judgment' Osborne. Conversely their heroes are not copybook heroes. One looks forward with eagerness to the next volumes of this history, which looks like being worthy of its subject.

Industrial Relations Journal

'A great deal of new information is provided'

William McCarthy

This monumental introduction to the history of Britain's largest and most fascinating union runs to almost a thousand pages: some 500,000 words have been required to take us to the point where the amalgamation began on the first of January 1922. One must admire the devotion of students, or union members, who work their way through to the end.

In his wry and modest foreword, the union's departing General Secretary, Ron Todd, insists that 'This background history had to be done, so that we can start to understand how the "One Big Union" amalgamation of 1922 actually came into being'. Of course he is quite right: one cannot wish that Coates and Topham had begun with the dock strike of 1889, or even the later conflagration of 1912. What is inexplicable is why they did not choose, or were not compelled, to tell their story in less than half the words. What we have here is a discursive first draft which has somehow escaped the blue pencil. This is a great pity, for there is the basis for an admirable single volume; a great deal of new information is presented in a clear and well balanced way. Even as it stands, it is essential reading for all serious students of the labour movement.

Part One takes us to 1911 and is in some ways the more satisfactory. The focus throughout is on the unions which eventually came together to form the Transport Workers' Federation in 1910. The differences between dockers, teamers, watermen, horsemen and the rest are well described and analysed. The rival attractions of 'Sectionalism' or 'Generalism' are delineated with skill and sympathy. The strengths and weaknesses of 'Federation', as against full-scale 'Amalgamation', are perceptions outlined. (Similar considerations can be seen behind current attempts at greater unity in the union movement of today.)

A clear outline is traced from a 'new unionism' of the 1870s, via succeeding boom and slump, to the rise of the rank-and-file militance that produced the Great London Dock Strike of 1889 (arguably the most important dispute in the history of British trade unionism). The factors conducive to victory in 1889 are contrasted with those that led to the period of 'Defeat, Defence and Defiance' that followed. The book ends with the rebirth of confidence that precipitated the 'Big Bang' of 1911.

The explanations offered for 'success' or 'failure' are convincing and well argued throughout. The conditions of the labour and product market are allied to a complex network of social and political causation, including the role of union leadership. Perhaps the leading figures from the Pantheon of the left are treated with undue warmth and understanding – e.g. Mann, Tillett and Larkin. But they were, on the whole, more attractive and trustworthy than their opponents on the right – notably Tupper, Wilson and that shallow windbag Burns. Most refreshing of all, in an authorised trade union history, these people are seen as human beings. It is appreciated that trade union leadership has always been a tough trade, where membership ingratitude and the prospect of electoral defeat has seldom been far from the skyline.

Apart from its inordinate length, I have only two substantial criticisms to make. First, the treatment of the law is casual and superficial. In particular, there is no account of the way in which a whole series of judicial decisions combined to set aside the statutory protection which the unions thought they had obtained in 1871 and 1876 long before the Taff Vale judgment. As a consequence, there is no satisfactory explanation for the inclusion of Section 4 – which protected unions' actions in tort beyond the limits of a trade dispute – in the 1906 Trade Disputes' Act. Yet, in Bill Wedderburn's phrase, this 'belt and braces' provision was eminently justified in the light of previous 'judicial creativity'. It was also to prove of considerable benefit to the T&G in the years that followed. As it is, Sidney Webb's ignorant and wrong-headed verdict on section 4 is allowed to stand uncorrected.

Second, Coates and Topham go out of their way to include any evidence that appears to support Eric Hobsbawn in his attack on the first volume of Clegg, Fox and Thompson's *History of British Trade Unionism*, first published in 1967. *Aficionados* will recall that this intemperate assault mainly concerned how far the 'new unionism' first spotted by the Webbs was really 'new'. This fruitless argument proved to be partly a row about definitions, and partly a debate which turned on the assumed perceptions of long dead trade unionists who left no record of their views. One had hoped by now that it had been decently forgotten.

Fortunately, Part Two deals with more important matters throughout. It is concerned mainly with three crucial developments: the movement for 'wider unity' which ended in the collapse of the Triple Alliance; the unprecedented growth in union membership and density which began in the First World War and lasted until the post-war recession; and the protracted and occasionally bitter negotiations that were required to produce eighteen successful amalgamation ballots in 1921. In each case a great deal of new information is provided, not least about the growth of the system of industry-wide bargaining which came to dominate British industrial relations for the next fifty years.

Once again, my most important criticisms concern law and membership attitudes. Despite the fact that the 1922 amalgamation would not have been conceivable without the passage of the 1917 Trade Union Amalgamation Act – which eased ballot requirements – its provisions are dismissed in a few lines. There is also no account of the campaign for its introduction. Although union growth after 1915 was greatly assisted by the introduction of legally binding arbitration and other provisions of the Treaty Agreement, the role of the law in this regard is totally ignored.

More surprisingly still, in some ways, there is no attempt to explain the transformation in the attitudes of the unions and their members toward the war itself. As in virtually all past union histories, the authors appear to be baffled by the onset of what they termed the 'surge' of 'working-class patriotism'. Indeed, leaders such as Tillett, who moved as fast as their members in support for the war, are denounced because they became 'as bellicose as any Blimp'. By contrast, the more conditional approach of Bevin is approved of as more 'subtle judgement'. It is almost as if, by embracing what is termed 'vulgar patriotism', the rank and file of the labour movement have let their historians down; in any case the latter prefer to avert their eyes.

Yet there is much in Part Two to admire. The best chapters deal with Bevin's strategy before the Shaw Inquiry in 1920 and his role in persuading so many executives to back the amalgamation. There is also a valuable account of how he came to arrive at the constitutional principles embodied in the T&G rule book: that unique mixture of sectional safeguards and what Bevin liked to term the rules designed to promote 'the interests if the organic "ole"'.

What also appears is that even at this time the aim of this amazing man exceeded his grasp. It seems that he wished to bring into his amalgamation all the organisations that subsequently formed the basis of the NUGMW, as well as all the railway unions. One can only wonder at the consequences for the movement if he had succeeded! There might be now no need for a TUC! As ever, Bevin emerges from close study as a complex, ruthless and dominating figure: boundlessly self-confident and frankly terrifying. There is also further evidence that what gave him the final edge was a passion for logical argument. Bevin actually preferred persuasion; threats were employed only when rationality failed, and he despised those who succumbed to them. Once again, we have to thank the authors for a very human picture of the greatest union leader so far. One hopes that their candid approach will survive the arrival of the next six General Secretaries.

British Journal of Industrial Relations, June 1992

A thorough-going revisionist view

Nina Fishman

The Transport and General Workers' Union has been Britain's biggest and most influential union for as long as most of us can remember. Its difficult birth from the amalgamation of 18 different, often disparate unions was seen at the time as a triumph for the first general secretary, Ernest Bevin. Historians concurred with contemporary judgement.

This July, the T&G's 34th BDC (Biennial Delegate Conference) at Blackpool was Ron Todd's last conference as general secretary. He received a warm display of affection from delegates and a fulsome eulogy from Bill Morris, the general secretary-elect.

Todd and Morris come from the union's left wing, which has dominated its leadership since Frank Cousins gained the top office after the previous incumbent's sudden death. The T&G left wing shared other socialists' negative view of Bevin. He was anti-communist, undemocratic, and had done little to merit their respect. It was therefore remarkable and moving to hear Bill Morris accord

Ron Todd a place in the roll of venerable T&G general secretaries beginning with Ernest Bevin, and continuing through Frank Cousins, Jack Jones and Moss Evans. Morris expeditiously altered the actual line of succession by omitting the two general secretaries who were Bevin's immediate successors and keen Cold War crusaders!

Morris's revisionism is timely. The T&G may have weathered the coincidence of statutory attack and Britain's manufacturing atrophy, but Bill Morris faces an enormous task in guiding Britain's largest union back to it pre-eminent position in 'the movement'. The *FT* has regularly reported the political infighting within the union's executive; there are continuing financial difficulties. The union and its members need the self-confidence and conviction of both the justice and the importance of their cause which is Bevin's legacy.

Delegates to the BDC were given the first instalment of the T&G's official history. It is handsomely produced in a boxed set and covers the eventful period from the London Dock Strike in 1889 to the T&G's birth in the aftermath of the First World War ...

... One of the people who emerges unexpectedly from the mists of the past is Robert Williams. Williams is generally neglected because of his place in labour movement demonology for his alleged betrayal during Black Friday in 1921. Coates and Topham argue that his sentence is wholly unmerited, and report his capable and energetic leadership of the Transport Workers' Federation during the war ...

Coates and Topham take a thorough-going revisionist view of Ernest Bevin. While they make no attempt to conceal their own strong commitment to workers' control and industrial democracy, they chronicle fully the circumstances which led Bevin to become a centraliser. They also quote extensively from his early speeches and writings to show how in many ways his own views on the world coincide with their own principles.

They absolve Bevin from the notorious and familiar charges of ill-treatment of other union leaders, notably Ben Tillett. They acknowledge the 'negative' qualities of the man – the unusual force, bluntness, and overweening arrogance. But they do not accept the left's usual verdict that these qualities were *prima facie* evidence of Bevin's 'dictatorship'.

British trade unions have been no less affected by national characteristics than British business or British politics. Even when there have been marked upheavals and conflicts, and notable peaks and troughs in their development, they have usually invented a continuous tradition to prove their legitimacy. Coates and Topham have shown that the T&G is no exception to this strong desire for an authenticated past. Nevertheless readers will also find the evidence which gives authenticity to this presumption of continuity.

Certainly, the spirit and the culture, which the force of Bevin's character infused into the institution he founded, were still very much in evidence at the union's BDC in July 1991. Instead of the barely concealed holiday atmosphere which accompanies British conventions held by the sea, the delegates were disciplined and serious-minded. They came to the rostrum to proclaim to all the world (whom they assumed to be listening) the dilemmas and injustices faced in their workplaces.

Bevin moulded the T&G in the belief that his union would make history. The delegates in Blackpool still behave as if they were people of destiny. Reading the official history can only reinforce their sense of having been called to serve 'their' and Bevin's people.

Financial Times, 26 September 1991

'Will be thumbed over by historians for years to come'

Lewis Minkin

This is the beginning of an enormous and impressive project in trade union history. 850 pages (in two parts) gets us to the birth of the Transport and General Workers' Union in 1922 but, in the process, the authors explore deep into the roots of the various forces and elements which made up the amalgamated union, and the context is given to us with such richness that at times it amounts almost to a history of the British working class and its industrial and political organizations since 1870. The sub-title, 'The Emergence of the Labour Movement', gives us a fair sense of what this volume is really about.

The probing backwards and outwards has its dangers in terms of conveying the core organisational history. Coates and Topham have a deep love of the international labour movement and, at times, they find it difficult to resist the temptation to explain in great detail an important movement here, a significant tributary there, or even an interesting event over there. What saves this from becoming a distracting indulgence is the sheer quality of it all – sensitive, analytical, scholarly, and always beautifully written, sometimes with controlled passion.

As they explore this broad canvas, they are not afraid to plunge full-frontal into one historical controversy after another. What they have to say is of such value that it will be thumbed over by historians for many years to come.

At the centre of Part I is a particularly thorough exploration of New Unionism and its significance for the industrial and political trajectory of British Labour. There is also a fascinating piece of detective work concerning the influence of the new unions on the famous resolution of the 1899 TUC which led to the creation of the Labour Representation Committee. And throughout the volume there is a very illuminating exposition of the tensions between organised labour and the Liberal Party – particularly the conflict with Liberal employers, beginning with Bryant and May. As for the amalgamation manoeuvres and negotiations, these are presented here in detail for the first time, and with a subtle understanding of the numerous problems of securing an agreed organisational framework.

Overall, the story moves from the period when 'whole sections of the Victorian underclass of the poorest employees flocked to the new organisations in their hundreds of thousands', through the formation of the Labour Party, to the period when the new party became the official Opposition, and the elements of the TGWU were cemented into the amalgamated union. What Coates and Topham provide us with, in the process, is not simply a chronological, historical and an exploratory account; it is an educational tour, with valuable insights into a range of facets of trade unionism.

The paradoxes they uncover are numerous. *Freedom* exercised through collective strength in the face of the employers has always been labour's fundamental industrial purpose, but a section of the working class always had more than a little sympathy for freeing labour from trade unionism – or, at least, some of the features of its active strength. *Sectionalism* is a major problem, retarding the creation of the new union and its pursuit of national and international goals, but sectionalism is often the anchorage of committed trade unionism and the basis of an organisational democratic pluralism. *Recognition* is an act of the employer – an expression of the employer's willingness to negotiate. But it is also the way that trade unionists better understand their own collective identity.

Their reflections and asides amount almost to a running commentary on the prudential skills of trade union leadership within the different dimensions in which that leadership is exercised. Thus, whilst direct action and the pursuit of a range of ambitious political projects dominate the rhetoric in the period following the First World War, and draw our historical attention now, in this analysis we are also reminded that behind these epic conflicts major progress is being made by negotiation of more orthodox union aims. A bedrock of industrial relations practice is founded upon the new Joint Industrial Committees and the retention or registration of trade union recognition. With it go the achievement of shorter hours and the defence of war-time wage levels.

The Matchgirls Strike of 1885, the Docks Strike of 1889, the Manningham Mills Strike of 1890, and countless other industrial actions are presented in full colour, in their heroism, in their evocation of support and in their far-reaching consequences. But there is also a well-argued defence of Robert Williams, the historic scapegoat of Black Friday (especially on the Communist Left) – a union leader here seen as having the courage to vote not to proceed with a strike which might be disastrous. And we get a deep appreciation – particularly in the character of Bevin – that in the day-to-day life of trade union leaders, courage is often the willingness to stand up for 'the organic whole', for the best available compromise, for the husbanding of a strength which will allow the next action to be pursued effectively, and for a broad strategic view of the securing of trade union objectives.

The fundamental lesson of this volume is how a far-sighted and innovative, if at times ruthless, industrial leadership managed to pull together a range of diverse sections within a unified structure which advanced the interests of all of them. It is a message with international as well as national implications. Indeed, the crucial sub-text of the history presented here is that of the past channelling of energies within a limiting national theatre and the need for a new opening-out in the 1990s. The preoccupation is with a new emphasis on international trade unionism. And the vision is, in a sense, of One Big Union which can organise effectively on a global scale in order to cope with development of multinational capital and a range of new economic, environmental and political problems.

In furtherance of this vision, the authors attempt to draw out and re-establish from the legacy of early twentieth-century trade unionism an old tradition of internationalist democracy. At times, they perhaps over-emphasise its past strengths in Britain and understate the commitment to national Parliamentary institutions before 1918. Certainly, the culture of the British Labour Movement has always involved a powerful strain of national insularity and, until very recently, a lack of interest in European developments. Some of that is being shaken off, and there is a new interest in the building of international industrial and political linkage. Coates and Topham here give us some major assistance. In the pursuit of a new international labour movement we can take heart from this story of the birth of the Transport and General Workers' Union out of disparate sectional elements and distinctive traditions, and under circumstances of considerable adversity.

European Labour Forum (Spring 1992)

'Are we to see the growth of another form of New Unionism?'

Geoffrey Stuttard

... The book is clearly in a different league from the authors' previous publications on trade unions and industrial democracy, but their stance is still the same. They are both committed to the importance of trade unionism in British and international life, and, as members of the Institute for Workers' Control, to ways in which 'ordinary people' can and should have more power over their own and national life.

But they have never before had or taken the opportunity to delve deeply into some of the origins of late 19th-century trade unionism, and through this, to justify some of their previous claims that working people were capable of developing imaginative and unexpected responses to complicated and seemingly overwhelming problems.

This 'delving' is fitting for ex-mineworker Coates, and research into the run-up to the famous 1889 Dock Strike fitting for Topham, with his base in the important dockland areas of Hull and the North-East. But, here again, 1889 (often cited as the key event – 'The Match to Fire the Thames' – when match girls' and dockers' action led to the growth of the 'New Unionism' of general workers), is shown to have been preceded by more activity and organisation than previously emphasised.

So the book starts in 1870, moving through the detailed and involved stages up to the formation of the 'One Big Union' in 1922.

On the way, the story takes in the 1889 Dock Strike, and the emergence of the 'New Unionism', based not on the sometimes élite craft unions, but on the so-called unskilled but not unintelligent male and female workers in the wide variety of trades and grades of the time. The story moves on to the development of the Labour Party at the turn of the century and the transport workers' role in it, the formation of the National Transport Workers' Federation (the NTWF), and 'the Great Unrest' of 1911, with 'the Big Bang' of the transport workers' strike which heralded the industrial upheaval which preceded the outbreak of war in 1914.

That ends part one of the history, and part two is the account of how the NTWF developed from a federation of unions into the amalgamation of 1922, when originally 14 out of 22 unions balloted, voted to form 'the One Big Union', the T&GWU.

The key events known before are still the key events in this volume, but much thickened out by local and regional detail, as in the organisation of dockworkers outside London before and after 1889, all in a 'warts and all' manner which obtains throughout the book. And the 'heroes and heroines', are they still the same? Yes, Annie Besant, Ben Tillett, Tom Mann, Will Thorne and Harry Gosling are all there, but set in the rich context of the thoughts and actions of hundreds of previously unsung cast. Ernest Bevin gains in stature already in this history, well in advance of his later fame, and quite apart from his acclaimed and hilarious performance in the 1920 Shaw inquiry.

So how should the book be judged? It is one-sided history, but then, what is not? The authors make no secret of their bias, and enable the reader to see more clearly than before the evidence to support their case. The publication of the work could hardly be more appropriate at a hundred years or so from the union's foundations. The T&GWU may be entering still another phase, with the election of Bill Morris as general secretary, who happens to be black, and in a context of new challenges after a period of declining membership and political opposition. The challenges are not a mirror of those of the 1880s, but exhibit some of that decades characteristics – of unions trying to emerge from a slump, with millions of unskilled and deskilled yet intelligent workers either unemployed or on part-time or short-term contracts. Are we to see the growth of another form of 'New Unionism'?

The Times Higher Educational Supplement, 1 November 1991

'Profoundly refreshing'

Geoffrey Goodman

The history of British trade unionism was, and remains, a 'magnificent journey' in which, as Francis Williams concluded in 1954, the trade union movement had 'brought the whole nation with it on its journey'.

Since 1979, perhaps even before that watershed year, the trade union 'journey' has been traduced, ridiculed, diminished to the sidelines, especially by those who have never cared or bothered to consult history. Only the contemporary inadequacies of a beleaguered movement have effectively been drawn to public notice.

So it is profoundly refreshing, as well as illuminating, to have the tables turned, if only a little, by a new history which provides a superbly researched canvas of events leading up to the formation of the country's largest trade union, the Transport and General Workers' Union. Ken Coates and Tony Topham, always an impressive partnership, have embarked on the history of the TGWU with a dedication that will eventually characterise their work as an outstanding chronicle in the library of trade union affairs ...

This is the story about the *nature* of trade union struggle, not only against exceptionally tough and ruthless employers, but also often against dubious, if not openly corrupt, leadership in some of the early unions. Even the birth of the Labour Party failed to curb their chaotic proliferation and sectional divisions ...

This marvellous feast is the story about the sinews of the Labour Movement; and I hope profoundly that it will be produced in cheaper editions so that those who have grown up in contemporary times will be able to buy the story of a heritage which belongs to us all.

Tribune, 30 August 1991

'Clearly written and very readable'

Philip S. Bagwell

A reviewer's first impression of this history if that the authors have been too verbose. Surely it was not necessary to take over 900 pages to record what amounts to the pre-history of the T&GWU? The impression is quickly dispelled. The account is clearly written and very readable. It will be helpful to those using the book for reference that the chapters are divided into headed sections and that statements are well documented.

With reference to outstanding events in the half-century after 1870 the authors explain how the T&G came to be a general rather than industrial union. Early attempts to organise labour on the Thames estuary failed through inability to control the labour supply. A small nucleus of skilled tradesmen, such as stevedores, lightermen and coal trimmers were better paid and more regularly employed, but the vast impoverished mass of unskilled and casually employed labourers were widely regarded as unorganisable. There were plenty of redundant gas workers available in summer and agricultural labourers in winter to swamp the labour market.

Strikes during the upswing of the trade cycle in 1889 helped secure London-based and other dockers their 'tanner' an hour. Union membership soared. Union leaders realised that to prevent erosion of the hard-won gains of the boom they must 'reach out' to control the flood of cheap labour into the docks. By 1892 Tom Mann had organised eleven 'agricultural' branches of the dockers' union in the Humberside area alone. The amalgamation of the National Union of Agriculture and the Allied Workers with the T&GWU in 1982 was the culmination of a long-established link. Nearly a hundred years earlier the leaders of waterside unions had concluded that the successful organisation of the workforce involved recruiting, in a general union, all potential sources of waterside labour.

The establishment of the Shipping Federation in 1890, with its organisation of 'free labour' to smash strikes on shipboard and in the docks, and the slump in trade in the early 1890s persuaded union leaders of the need for greater co-ordination of their efforts. There were separate unions of dockers on Merseyside and in Scotland and South Wales, and dozens of locally based unions of carters. Regional wage settlements undermined effective national organisation. The National Transport Workers' Federation was therefore established in 1911 in the hope that it would encourage co-operation in nationwide action. In the event the Federation achieved very little control over its affiliated bodies. By this time outright amalgamation between transport unions was seen as the only worthwhile objective, but the conference organised for the purpose was cut short by the outbreak of war in August 1914.

Messrs Coates and Topham see the First World War as the 'devilish forcing ground' in which the main features of present-day industrial relations were shaped. Certainly the drive for 'One Big Union' in transport, with nationally based negotiations on wages and working conditions, was intensified and the T&GWU, compromising 18 amalgamated unions, started life on 1 January 1922.

In March 1919 the council of the National Transport Workers' Federation had a visionary ideal for the future. It demanded the creation of a National Board of Communications 'with equal representation of the employees and the state, which shall take over and administer the whole of the inland passenger, mail and goods transport of the country – road, rail, air and water – in the interests of the nation'. This plan proved impossible of fulfilment. The membership of the ASRS – precursor of the NUR – voted against affiliation with the NTWF in 1910. In contrast with employment in many other areas of transport, jobs on the railways were relatively secure; ties with the railway companies were increased with the introduction of the conciliation schemes in 1907 and 1911, and after the formation of the NUR in 1913 a large majority of railway workers were unionised. Certainly the NUR joined with the miners and the transport workers in the Triple Alliance of 1913, but following its successful strike in opposition to wage cuts in 1919 its members were reluctant to exchange the apparent security of a policy of industrial unionism for what seemed to be the greater risks of involvement in general unionism.

The seamen also stood aloof. The right-wing xenophobia of J. Havelock Wilson, the General Secretary of the National Sailors' and Firemen's Union, was at odds with the socialism and the internationalism of the leaders of the other transport unions. By 1910 Wilson had reached an accommodation with the leading shipping companies. In 1917, the government and the shipowners, concerned to ensure the flow of supplies to the war zones, set up the National Maritime Board, which included representatives from Wilson's union and the Ship Steward's union. The authors of this book describe the seamen's union as the 'Achilles heel' of the Transport Workers' Federation between 1911 and 1917, after which Wilson severed all links with the leaders of the other transport unions.

The failure to encompass railway workers and seamen in the T&G had important consequences for industrial relations in the transport industry after 1922. Although both the NUR and the T&G supported the general strike in 1926 the seamen's union did not.

The refreshing zeal of the authors for the ideal of One Big Union permeates their writing, but it does not cloud their critical judgement. They deplore the campaigns of the early twentieth century against the employment of Chinese labour on ships, describing it as 'a sign of the corrupting legacy of empire'. They consider that 'the passions unleashed in this unsavoury racist lobby were to do damage to many of those who took part in it'.

There are valuable pen portraits of both the leading protagonists and the rank and file in these industrial struggles. Ernest Bevin is revealed as a singleminded worker of prodigious energy. Harry Gosling, the first president of the TGWU, is described as 'honest but peremptory'. The perceptive wit of the dockers appears in the nicknames given to their foremen: 'Rembrandt', who says, 'Let me put you in the picture, men' and 'the Sheriff', who asks, 'Where's the hold-up lads?'

The poor quality of some of the illustrations and, in particular, the miniscule scale of the picture of those attending the foundation conference in 1921, do not do justice to the book.

The Journal of Transport History

'An authoritative history'

Denis Smyth

Although there has been several studies and important biographies of TGWU leaders, Ernest Bevin, and Frank Cousins, there has not been a detailed and comprehensive history of the union – up until now that is. The study by Tony Topham and Ken Coates is indeed an authoritative history of the biggest union to enter the industrial and political arena as 'one big union'. The book will become a standard in the history of trade unionism for years to come.The authors have performed a Herculean task in documenting the origins, growth and development of the T&G up to the amalgamation in 1922. They have still much to tell. It is indeed a brilliant study of trade union pioneers in the formative years – the Match Girls of 1888 and the Dockers of the 1889 Dock Strike. The study is crammed full of references, facts, graphics and tables to enable readers to follow the formation and development of the union.

Both Ken Coates and Tony Topham, with lucid and consummate

skill, plot the early days of the forerunners to amalgamation to the birth of the Transport and General Workers' Union. The TGWU played a special role in the history of trade unionism; one has only to look at the historic labour leaders who were in its early ranks.If one looks for a base-point, an explosion of unskilled labourers reaching for organisation, one can see the Dock Strike of 1889 as the spark that caused the eruption. For many courageous and skilful individuals played a vital and heroic role in the creation of what was to become the TGWU. It was out of the Dock Strike that the need for unity and organisation became apparent.

The authors of this book show how the TGWU was formed out of industrial conflict and battles, from the Dock Strike of 1889 to the Liverpool Transport Strike of 1911, through to many strikes in between, with the 1920 Docks Enquiry acting as catalyst. Two years after this enquiry the T&G was born and organised labour had arrived.

Unity, August 1991

'About the future as much as the past'

Walter Greendale

It is extraordinary that Britain's largest union, which is also the heir to the finest radical socialist traditions of new unionism, has waited so long to feature as the hero of a major work of labour history. Now, with the publication of Coates' and Topham's monumental study, the serious gap is beginning to close. The quality, as well as the size of this book, is worthy of the scale of the subject, and its appearance could not be more timely. For the TGWU, as well as the model of politically committed democratic unionism which it represents, is under severe challenge today.

The decision to devote a whole book to the origins of the Union, and to the long process of convergence to amalgamation of the transport and general labourers' unions, was a bold one. But the result justifies it. What Coates and Topham demonstrate is that the roots of the union reach back, in unbroken continuity, to the basic struggle of the very poorest people of late-Victorian Britain, to throw off their status as a despised under-class, and to transform themselves from a mob into a movement.

From that beginning, in the docks and tenements of Britain's major ports, the new unions of the so-called 'unskilled' reach out for wider and wider unity, in a prolonged struggle to overcome sectional and regional loyalties, in the quest for One Big Union. For this purpose, they not only used the mass strike, in 1889, and again in 1911, but also drove consistently for the goal of recognition, for national bargaining rights, and for political representation, in parliament and in local government. In the process, it was they, and not beneficent Liberal or Tory politicians, who created our national democracy, in the teeth of ferocious, often violent, opposition from employers and state. That is why the authors insist that as they formed the structure of modern trade unionism, the founders of the TGWU were also creating the modern labour movement.

It is an exciting story, told with a wealth of human and biographical detail, entirely committed yet honest and scholarly. Reading it, I was never bored, always carried on by the drive of the narrative. The almost mythical figures of Ben Tillett, Tom Mann, James Larkin, Jimmy Sexton, Harry Gosling, Bob Williams, and Ernest Bevin, and a host of others, come wonderfully to life, round, full personalities; neither sentimentalised nor stereotyped. They were a very great generation of leaders, 'warts and all', and their members displayed a courage and commitment – particularly through severe slumps and employers' counter-attacks – to match anything that the world of trade unionism has ever known.

At the climax, as Bevin and his colleagues laboured mightily on the final stages, the amalgamation of 18 unions, I was left feeling that I had witnessed a miracle of history. For 1921-2 were years of deep slump, and those 18 unions overcame a history of sectional rivalries in the most difficult circumstances, to form a tough but uniquely flexible structure which has stood the test of time.

Trade unions always face choices; of strategy, structure, and politics. Big daring choices were made then; this study is a challenge and a tool of analysis for our own generation, not a piece of nostalgia. It is about the future, as much as it is about the past.

Ken Coates and Tony Topham have been presenting challenges to our movement for many years, in their works on trade unionism and industrial democracy. As a member of the union's General Executive, over most of those years, and a former Chairperson, I am pleased that our union has backed this study without imposing any conditions on the authors.

Morning Star, June 1991

One Big Union

Michael Barratt Brown

This is a big book in every respect[1] ... The sub-title is not a false claim; it is a book about the emergence of the Labour Movement in Britain between 1870 and 1922. It could have been called 'The Making of the British Labour Movement'. For, it is a true sequel to Edward Thompson's *Making of the English Working Class*. It takes the story on from the 1870s to the early 1920s and it widens the focus to comprise the struggles of labour for a common identity and solid organisation in Scotland, Wales and Ireland as well as England. If the canvas is broad, this is not just because the Transport and General Workers' Union was formed from such a multitude of little local and sectional unions, but because a Labour Movement and a Labour Party in Britain had to be built, and was built in these years, from a collective consciousness generated in a thousand local and sectional struggles. It is entirely timely that this history should appear at the moment when the very idea of a Labour *Movement* is under question.

The future role of the trade unions in Britain, and especially of their relations with the Labour Party, which was their creation, is once more an issue of great importance. This link between industrial and political movements is an issue not only in British but also in European politics. Where is the collective consciousness of a European Labour Movement? Do workers need industrial organisations other than professional associations to look after their interests in modern society? If so, do they need to combine in industrial unions or in a single national organisation like the TUC to provide a common strategy for labour, and a negotiating force with government? If so, how should they relate to a political party in Parliament, representative of the wider interests of Labour? How then should they establish international links with other national organisations of Labour and other socialist parties? Is there still a general interest of Labour as opposed to that of Capital as would need a Labour Movement? Or have all the other interests – of nation, gender, race and religion – come to assume more importance in the need that men and women perceive for uniting to defend themselves against oppressive powers?

It is the very direct link between the founding of the TGWU and the emergence of a Labour Movement in Britain that Ken Coates and

Tony Topham want us to understand in this monumental history of the Union. Together they have made such major contributions to our understanding of the history and structure of British trade unions and to their democratic development in the last three decades that this history must arouse the immediate interest of all who are concerned with the present and future of the British Labour Movement. Readers will not be disappointed, although they may be somewhat daunted by the length of the two-part first volume, which takes the story only up to 1922, when the TGWU was founded. In many ways, the struggles of Labour in those years to find a voice and a presence were to set the mould of British politics for a century. Many of the same questions which are being asked today in a European and world-wide perspective were being asked and answered a hundred years ago, in the movement for One Big Union.

The Role of Unions – Then and Now

There are striking similarities between the 1880s and 90s, and our own times. The world's industrial economies were just emerging from the low point of the 70s and 80s, then as now, in the long-term trade cycle. As a central element in the cycle, economies were having to adapt to revolutionary technological change. Then it was electric power and the internal combustion engine, while today it is the computer and the new information technology. Such change was, and is, massively labour-saving, rendering obsolete nearly all existing labour skills and forms of labour relations. Capital was then, as now, going through a radical process of restructuring and rationalisation in combines and amalgamations, on a national and international scale. New national centres of capital accumulation were emerging to challenge the old. Then it was in Germany and the USA, as today it is Japan, South Korea and other newly industrialising countries. How should workers respond to such a world turned upside-down?

Of course, there are crucial differences between the two periods. Standards of living, at least in the industrial countries, have radically altered. There are fewer today in Britain who are starving and homeless. There is comprehensive education, a universal health service, widespread income support in sickness, unemployment and old age. Trade unions in these same countries have become a part of the establishment. Women have gained a voice, albeit still limited, in the unions and the Labour Party. Suffrage is universal for all men and women over the age of 18. There have been long periods of Labour in government, There is a European Parliament, and an Assembly of the United Nations. Many of these beneficial changes were struggled for by the founders and forerunners of the One Big Union, and can be attributed to their struggles. Nor are they small matters to be derided. Some have required continual struggle to maintain. Others have lost some of their cutting edge, and are in need of sharpening to protect the interests of the most disadvantaged and underprivileged in society.

It was for the underclass, and especially the dockers, the outcast 'people of the abyss' for whom the little band of socialists and social reformers fought in 1880s, and made the dockers 'tanner' into a great moral issue in 1889. It was not just the money that mattered, but recognition of the workers' bargaining rights, of a limit to hours and demands of work, of some permanence of employment, a degree of control by the unions over the daily scramble at the dock gates for a day's work. Some of the early leaders in the docks like Burns and Mann came from union organisation outside the abyss and their support from still further afield – Annie Besant, Charles Booth, Cardinal Manning, Eleanor Marx, Beatrice Webb. Coates and Topham rescue Mann from his critics to reveal the most imaginative socialist and committed organiser linking the ILP and the unions. They remind us, further, that the trade union movement in Britain was built by socialists: three-fifths of the delegates to the TUC in 1898 belonged to the ILP, and a motion in favour of support for the 'working class parties' was emphatically carried. The second generation of leaders – Bevin, Clynes, Connolly, Larkin, Williams – were not the less socialists because they came from the ranks of the outcasts themselves to create the big unions out of the new non-craft unionism of the 1890s.

More than this, the message that Coates' and Topham's study carries for us is that the historians who have noted only the middle-class leaders involved in the Great Dock Strike have missed the essential point. The 'dock rats' had become the 'new unionists', turning 'whole lifetimes of personal subjection and defeat into a wild joy of collective triumph'. They quote Olive Schreiner (not just a 'novelist' as she is described) writing to Edward Carpenter in 1889, when the dockers in their thousands marched through the West End of London in perfect order to converge on Hyde Park, the first such rally since the 1860s: 'You look straight into their faces and their eyes look back at you; they are possessed with a large idea ... I never felt so full of hope'. But would it be large enough to bury sectionalism and build a movement?

The central themes of this first volume of the Transport and General Workers' history that are followed by Coates and Topham are at one level the battle against sectionalism, but at another deeper level the battle for recognition for the collective identity of Labour. The struggle against sectionalism has been revealed before, but not in the depth of detail and essential continuity discovered here. In Britain at the turn of the century every trade had its union, and nearly every port or city its own 'national' amalgamated associations. There were 29 waterfront unions in the Port of London alone in 1912. Yet, Coates and Topham are able to show that, contrary to the received wisdom of the historians of industrial relations, it was the unions' organisation that forced the employers to organise, and not the reverse. They quote the 1894 Royal Commission on Labour as saying, 'Formal organisations of employers usually make their appearance at a later date than those of the workmen and arise for purpose of joint resistance, when the individual employers find themselves too weak to cope with the growing strength of trade unions'. The Shipping Federation, which was to have such a violent history in the shipping industry, was formed in 1890, immediately after the Great Dock Strike and its sequel in the great recruiting tour of Southern, Welsh and Eastern ports which Burns and Mann made together in 1889-90. Coates and Topham show, further, that it was only when Bevin and the National Transport Workers' Federation had the port employers on the ropes at the Shaw Inquiry in 1920, and Shaw recommended a national standard rate and the formation of a National Joint Industrial Council for the industry, that the port employers established their counterpart, National Federation of Port Employers.

Trade union unity was, nonetheless, hard won and the employers were generally able to override their own market competition to make common cause against their workers, when the trade unions felt strong enough to press their demands in a period of boom. And the employers had little difficulty in staying together, to divide and conquer the men, as soon as the boom turned to slump. There was always a great reserve army of labour available as blacklegs, drawn from the country, from the unemployed and forever replenished from Ireland, from China, from India and, when the employers had government support in wartime, from the armed forces. It was a miracle of organisation and patient negotiation that made possible the foundation of the Transport and General Workers' Union from the eighteen founding unions in the middle of the post-war slump of

1921-27; and it is to this 'Grand Movement' that the two parts of this volume inevitably progress.

Syndicalism and the New Unions

Coates and Topham are able to show a clear line of advance of the new unionism, despite many setbacks and defeats between 1870 and 1922. They demonstrate convincingly that the explosion of strikes in British ports in 1911 was no spontaneous combustion, but the end result of forty years of struggle and organisation. With all their weaknesses, leaders like John Burns, Tom Mann and Ben Tillett in London, James Larkin in Ireland, James Sexton in Liverpool, Joseph Houghton in Glasgow, and Havelock Wilson of the Seamen's Union, are revealed again and again trying to give a true leadership to rank and file movements, struggling for recognition; not just of workers' rights, but of their very humanity, protecting their fragile organisations under attack, daring all when their members were driven into revolt, balancing always Labour's demand for independence of capital with the need for recognition by capital. If some became Government ministers like Burns, dined like Tillett at Frascatis on champagne, became wartime patriots like Sexton, or reached for their guns like Larkin, or relied like Havelock Wilson on the employers for a closed shop, their defence of their members was generally unwavering, often imaginative, and sometimes downright heroic. Although they became increasingly Parliamentary figures rather than union activists, some, at least, of the reforming zeal of the Asquith and Lloyd George Governments can be attributed to them. That the central core of conviction in the 'New Unionism' was syndicalist was due to the continuing influence of Tom Mann's writings, of Bevin's advocacy and extra-Parliamentary organisation and skills, and of Bob Williams' persistent appeals for union activity in the *Weekly Record,* which he edited.

The new unions undoubtedly looked to governments for legislation to protect, rather than destroy, the gains they made in collective bargaining, but the strength which they sought, in place of the defence of craft skills, lay in numbers. The low subscription rate, the absence of benefits except for strike pay, the principle of general recruitment, the pursuit of collective bargaining and the endless search by way of joint committees and federations to achieve strength through unity, all attest to the faith in numbers. 'One Big Union' was the aim, not just to earn better wages for the unskilled and semi-skilled, but to win recognition, the right to bargain – for shorter hours of work, health and safety standards, and an ever widening extension of workers' control over the process and product of work. Coates and Topham show that the key structure in their strategy was the Joint Industrial Council, which emerged from the First World War as a result of the Whitley Committee report, and came therefore to be known as Whitleyism.

The Joint Industrial Councils provided a forum for bargaining between employers and workers' representatives in a whole industry. In 1917, they were seen by the Government as a response to widespread industrial unrest and rising prices, falling real wages and profiteering, particularly in engineering. But it was in the industries characterised by having male manual labour in which the craft element was minimal, that they became most firmly established – cement, chemicals, chocolate manufacture, flour milling, fertilisers, rubber, sugar refining, etc. And these were just the ones in which the new general unions had deepest roots. To these were added the public sector establishments. In all, the Councils gave to the unions the industry-wide and nation-wide scope to develop and exercise a united presence. Some union leaders were suspicious of state incorporation; others saw in the Councils the basis for the Guild Socialist objective of control of industry by the workers themselves. For Bevin and Williams and the Transport Workers they were a means to an end – the achievement of national organisation and coordination over a wide range of workers, combining at once both centralisation of power, and decentralisation of action. They enabled the extension of the Transport Workers' power into the general unions of other industries. Bevin even saw them as an instrument of workers' control in continuing war-time allocations of scarce raw materials.

The meaning of recognition

Recognition for the dockers and the unions in and around Britain's ports meant more than recognition of the right to bargain with employers and governments. The struggle for recognition provides the second main theme which runs through this study. It meant self-recognition, first of all, which employers and governments had to accept; but this carried with it something more important, the dignity and strength of a collective presence in a society where a small élite had narrowly defined itself as representative of the whole of 'society'.

To get the feel of it, one has to compare it to the extreme form of alienation of black people in South Africa. Today in Britain, where such extremes seem to most people to be quite remote, it is these very foundations of a self-conscious Labour Movement and working class that are under challenge. Mrs Thatcher's class instinct was wholly right to lead her to deny that there was such a thing as society, but only families and individuals, if society was to include the whole people. For, she was not only denying the rich pluralism of associations for a thousand purposes, which make up civil society, she was denying the collective consciousness of those who stand outside a quite narrow élite in a country like Britain.

What the dockers and their allies were creating at the beginning of the century was a new perception of themselves in response to the way their masters perceived them. Recognition registered that perception. For, they were not merely climbing out of the 'abyss', they were creating a movement of Labour which could claim to challenge the hegemony of the ruling élite. If socialists created the first unions, it was their collective action that created the Labour Party. It is a matter of crucial importance for our own times that a *Labour Party – the* Labour Party – is nothing if it fails to reflect the way that those who are not part of the élite perceive themselves as a collectivity, and not just as men and women, black and white, Scots, Welsh, Irish, English, etc. When the major achievements of this collective action are at risk – a comprehensive school system, a universal health service, adult education, social security, public housing – its validity can hardly be denied. The appeal at the beginning of the century was to a sense of class. At the end of the century, it may have to embrace our common humanity, perhaps as a first step our Europeanness, as people with common interests and purposes which go largely unrecognised by the European élite. Their recognition of our presence will again require and involve the recognition of ourselves as a collective force. It is indeed timely to be reminded of the way such collectivity was established.

Building the Union for Labour

How and by whom the Labour Movement in Britain would be led when it reached out from economic to political power, was unclear in the early 1920s. Coates and Topham give equal credit to Bevin and Williams in the founding of the Transport and General Workers' Union, but it was Bevin who was to carry it forwards after 1922.

Williams's name was almost forgotten in the history of the period, and it was Bevin who delivered the Union to the Labour Party. This was not predetermined. War was the midwife to great new births as well as the cause of millions of dead. In the chapters on 1914-18 and in the following chapter on '1919', Coates and Topham show how Bevin and Williams, acting for the Transport Workers' Federation, sought in industry after industry to capitalise the gains of the war years – in shorter hours and enhanced weekly and overtime rates of wages. The dockers were the last to be tackled, but in the Shaw Inquiry, Bevin won the principle of de-centralisation and a guaranteed minimum income, financed jointly by the employers and the state, and union control over discipline. It was a Pyrrhic victory. The slump of 1921, especially affecting foreign trade, brought the employers back to the offensive. Men were laid off, wages were cut, the unity of the unions in the federation broken up.

From the position of strength which enabled Bevin to rally the Triple Alliance of miners, railwaymen and dockers to threaten direct action against the Government's warlike moves of intervention in the Russian Revolution, the Transport Workers found themselves reduced to local negotiations with employers, and divided by misunderstanding and narrow sectionalism from the other members of the Triple Alliance. It was not just a miracle that Bevin succeeded, in 1922, in fusing together the eighteen union associations which formed the founding members of the Transport and General Workers' Union, it was an immense tribute to the respect which Bevin had won for himself in so many struggles to keep together fellow members of the loosely built Transport Workers' Federation.

Coates and Topham have done much to rescue Bevin from the hagiography of the lone hero in Bullock's biography and his denigration by Communist historians. He is revealed as a brilliant strategist, capable of outwitting even Lloyd George. He is shown to have been the true instigator of the refusal to load *Jolly George* with arms for Russia; not Harry Pollitt, for whom this honour has often been claimed. Driven by a single-minded commitment to build self-confidence and unity among working people in a union which would stand the test of time and allow for sectional and regional differences within one common structure, he appears as both ruthless and humane. He dropped the Transport Workers' Federation to build the amalgamation on his own dockers' union, but won support as much by humane values and cultural sensitivity as by the sheer size of his fist

– a 'bunch of bananas', as Samuel Gompers described it. (For the first time I now understand why my father, a Quaker pacifist, philosopher and ILP member from 1912, was devoted to him, and worked for him as a welfare officer in the Ministry of Labour in World War Two – and not just because Bevin opposed conscription in 1916 and fought for the release of conscientious objectors like my father, who were still held in British jails in 1919.) Above all, it was into the Labour Party that Bevin took the big new union and not into a Social Democratic party or Communist party.

The fact, however, that Bevin built the T&G as a new organisation, but on the strong base of his own Union, and not as a centralised form of the Transport Workers' Federation, means that the force and quality of Bob Williams's contribution to the Labour Movement as Secretary of the Federation from 1912 to 1921 has been overlooked. Coates and Topham establish Williams as a genius of an audacious initiative, and a man of tireless energy. His single-handed editing of the *Weekly Record* led the field in trade union journals – no other appearing more frequently than monthly – and his tours of unions and branches throughout the United Kingdom gave to the Federation its inspiration, its marching orders and its reputation for encouraging joint action. But, at the crucial moment of history, Bob Williams was discredited. He was expelled from the Communist Party, of which he was a founding member, as a result of his part in the collapse of the Triple Alliance on 'Black Friday', April 15th 1921. In one blow, Williams lost his base and the Communist Party its leading trade unionist. Bevin more easily moved centre of the stage. Had Williams not been expelled, the Federation might have survived and the Communist Party would have had one member of real standing in the unions to claim the leadership of the Labour Movement. Coates and Topham effectively demolish the case against Williams, sedulously propagated by Communist writers – that the miners were betrayed by the other members of the Triple Alliance in 1921, when, in fact, they were themselves deeply divided and vacillated over proceeding with the strike, for which the Alliance had pledged support. But it was enough at the time that he was expelled.

Coates and Topham show Williams as a brilliant editor, inspiring speaker, robust advocate of amalgamation among transport and kindred workers, with a deep political commitment to democratic socialism, and an outstanding range of technical information. In 1913 he predicted coal power being followed by gas and oil, and finally superseded by 'atomic or molecular' energy. It was on this basis that he argued for one union. The miners would need their allies; the alliance must be democratically based, but with strong central power. Williams was Bevin's only rival for leadership of the new big union. With Williams discredited and the Federation shown to be too loose a structure for effective action, the way was open for Bevin's step by step amalgamation from his base in the Dockers' Union, among the port workers and the carters and cabbies, and the clerks and bus and tram drivers who surrounded the ports.

More than One Big Union

It was a miracle, the founding of the Transport and General Workers' Union in 1922, but it was not One Big Union (with or without capital letters), not even one union in transport. The National Union of Railwaymen declined the invitation to join. Jimmy Thomas probably saw to that, but his members undoubtedly preferred to hold on to its narrower form of a railway union with the promise for them of lifelong employment as railway servants. The seamen did not join. Havelock Wilson, the leader of the National Seamen's and Firemen's Union, the largest of the seamen's unions, would never have kow-towed to Bevin, and Bevin did not want the Amalgamated Marine Workers' Union, Manny Shinwell's breakaway Glasgow and Southampton based maritime union, to be constantly stirring the pot with Havelock Wilson. Most divisively, there emerged in the early 1920s not one, but two, big General Unions. The Municipal Employees Association and the Tyneside dockers in the National Amalgamated Union of Labour turned down the offer to amalgamate with the T&G in 1922, and instead joined with the Gasworkers (Thorne's union) and general labourers in the National Union of General Workers (NUGW), to form the General and Municipal Workers' Union. There had been rivalry between the NUGW and the Dockers' Union over access to dock work in London, and Bevin, after reaching agreement with James Sexton's National Union of Dock Labourers, discouraged a further dock workers' merger, other than with the clerical staff, concentrating rather on winning the vehicle, tramway, cab drivers' and carriers' unions.

Coates and Topham have performed an heroic task in unravelling a consecutive story from the minute books and union records, in a field where so many scholars have been content with the biographies, autobiographies and public statements of leaders. They have, thus, revealed the rich diversity of British union experience in every port in the British Isles; and in doing so, moreover, set the detailed story of struggles over forty years within a clear framework of the wider economic developments of the time – the periods of boom when labour was drawn in from the country, and the sharp slump when tens of thousands of men were laid off, creating a permanent reserve army of the unemployed; the expansion of empire encouraging a growth in the volume of Britain's foreign trade, moving well ahead of industrial output; the introductions of new transport technology – steam in place of sail, electric trams in place of coaches and cabs, and finally the internal combustion engine in place of horses and human carriers; the emergence of US and German industrial competition; and with it all, the increasingly unequal distribution of income and wealth as wages fell in their share of national income and the two extremes were exposed – a small *rentier* class, flaunting its wealth in the face of the mass of labourers, most markedly in the capital city, but outside London as well, in a country where five million received half the national income, leaving the other half to be shared between 38 million.

The Curse of Sectionalism

The question must remain, how it was that the largest proletariat of any individual nation, with the smallest intermediate class between capital and labour, failed to mount a stronger and more united challenge to the rule of capital. The answer is the curse of sectionalism – that is the thread which runs through all the detail of this volume. First, there was the hostile contempt for the unskilled among the aristocrats of labour, the craftsmen, themselves divided into a hundred sectional trades, which were to be challenged increasingly by technological change. Second only to that must be reckoned the nationalism of port organisations in England, Wales, Scotland and Ireland, and the sectarianism of Catholic and Protestant, whether in Ireland, Glasgow or Liverpool. Third, there was the exclusion of women from unions – almost from the book, despite the Match Girls who are celebrated and Mary MacArthur whose contribution to the National Federation of Women Workers is recognised in the Appendix, but were there no women among the shop assistants at Liptons and the Army and Navy Stores? Fourth, and ever present, was the racism which consciousness of the imperial power engendered, and which employers could exploit to head off common action with Chinese labour in the ports, or Lascars on the ships. The complex detail of Coates' and Topham's text makes these professional, national, sectarian and racial divisions clear enough, but they are not perhaps brought sufficiently into the centre of the vast picture that is drawn. Why was such sectionalism in Britain so much stronger than elsewhere, in Germany for example?

The precise relationship between Britain's early industrial supremacy, the imperial connection, and later industrial decline, has still to be finally teased out. Coates and Topham have provided rich materials for teasing, but much work remains to be done, perhaps in their second volume. I have argued elsewhere[2] that the proposition of a City-Empire-Treasury nexus at the end of the Nineteenth Century, holding back productive industry for the sake of financial and commercial stability, is deeply flawed. There is little evidence that British industry was starved of capital, but it was heavily oriented overseas. Outside London, banking links with industry have always been firmly established. State expenditure as a proportion of national income was well ahead of that of Britain's US and German rivals in the whole period of 1870-1914. Vast colonial power and the British naval presence throughout the world cannot be reconciled with the concept of a 'nightwatchman state'. Coates and Topham too readily accept the myth of a *laissez-faire* economy, and miss the central point about the size of Britain's transport industry.

The British transport industry, including half the world's shipping, whose predominant size in the late Nineteenth Century Coates and Topham rightly recognise, cannot be categorised as non-productive in Marx's sense, a point on which Marx himself insisted. But it was not manufacturing industry. The volume of Britain's foreign trade – imports and exports – was increasingly being sustained by overseas investment, which brought profits to the investors, and service incomes to the workers. The new manufacturing industries, based on electric power and the internal combustion engine, were slow to develop in Britain compared with what their rivals were doing. There was more money to be made for British capital overseas, in mining and plantations, and in railway construction and utilities; and in the one growth area at home – the transport industry – there was plenty of cheap labour to be had from declining agriculture, and especially from Ireland. Williams is quoted several times, complaining in the *Weekly Record of* the employers' lack of managerial capacity due to the tradition of reliance on a surplus of casual labour in the ports. So, the defensive sectionalism of the craftsmen in Britain's traditional industries sat all too comfortably beside an unenterprising management. It was in the USA, and not in Britain, that Ford's Model T factory was established in 1908. British employers went on relying on one-off production in a captive empire market, and on the use of cheap labour in transport and services.

It was highly significant that it was the Workers' Union, with its links via Tom Mann to the Transport Unions, and not the Engineers Union itself, which organised the semi-skilled workers of the new industries in the Midlands. The Engineers were defeated by the employers in 1897-8, trying to resist the displacement of traditional skills by mass production methods. Coates and Topham report that Tom Mann, himself an engineer, offered the job of organising the unskilled and semi-skilled workers in engineering to the Amalgamated Society of Engineers, but they turned the offer down. Industrial unionism did not develop in Britain. Only the miners' federation and the railway union, with a bare half of the transport industry, could be called industrial unions, and they failed to win over their most skilled sections – the overmen in mining, and the locomen on the railways. For this failure they would pay dear in the end – the miners in 1984-5 strike, and the railwaymen in 1978.

By contrast, German workers coming to industry directly into the new technology, found no difficulty in establishing industrial unions combining skilled, semi-skilled and unskilled grades. Those who visited Germany before the First World War, like G.D.H. Cole of the Guild Socialists and Williams and Gosling of the Transport Workers, came back duly impressed. But the model could not be copied – the semi-skilled workers in Britain came to be organised in general unions. It was a tribute to Tom Mann's Workers' Union, and to the Transport and General Workers' Union to which the Workers' Union adhered in 1929, that they were organised at all. While it was a great victory to achieve the amalgamation of the transport workers' unions (apart from sea and rail) and the many general unions in industry, to create what was, and remained, Britain's largest union, the TGWU was not the One Big Union which many who worked for it had dreamed of. The central lay authority of the TGWU and its regional offices and trade groups provided a powerful and democratic structure for advancing the cause of labour. But a general union falls short of an industrial union, both in its power at the workplace, and in its potential for pursuing a united and aggressive strategy with the employers, most particularly in relation to the introduction of new technology.

... The fact remains that it was not the strength of the trade unions that led to the failure of British industry to maintain its early competitive superiority; it was their weakness. In the 1922 amalgamation the T&G made the best of a bad job, but the message of Coates' and Topham's study is that the great achievement lay elsewhere, in the making of the British Labour Movement.

What then are we to say about the lessons to be drawn from this history for our own times? The power of capital remains, more concentrated, more international. Despite the growth of trade unions, workers inside nations and between nations remain divided, their power in relation to the giant concentrations of capital quite limited. Even governments of large nation states like the UK are no match for them. Regional and international institutions for regulating the market have hardly begun to replace the waning power of nation states. Yet, as a result of Labour Movement pressure, state intervention through social provision and social security has, in the last hundred years, done much to correct the worst features of a society in which profit was the supreme arbiter of the lives and condition of the people. Now, many of the gains of the unions in this century have been rolled back in Britain in the last two decades. Unemployment and a reserve army of labour are once more regarded as appropriate instruments of economic regulation. There is a growing number in the abyss of Britain's great cities today, to set beside the hundreds of millions in the shanty towns of the Third World, whose condition rivals what Charles Booth and Beatrice Webb described in London at the beginning of the century. Divisions in the ranks of Labour between skilled and unskilled, men and women, black and white, English and Irish, Protestant and Catholic, Muslim and Jew, are no less than a century ago. Perhaps they are even greater. It would need a Dr Pangloss to say that there is no longer the need for an overarching organisation of Labour, international and ecumenical. There is still much to be learned from the work of those who sought to build One Big Union which would have central power, but decentralised representation by trades and regions.

Beyond the question of the Big Union, however, there is the much bigger question of a Labour Movement. What does this phrase mean? It is not unique to British culture; most of Europe has its *Mauvements, Movimientos* and the like. They are not the same as Social Democracy or Democratic Socialism. In Britain the Movement was the basis for a Party of organised Labour. That is what this book is about. It did not happen by chance, but was made that way by the pioneers whose lives and acts are studied here. What, then, is a Movement? What is it that moves? One thing at least is clear; a movement cannot die, but must be capable of survival, unlike so many explosions of Labour protest that erupted in the United States, like volcanoes which fizzle out within a few years. The Webbs insisted that a trade union was 'a continuous association of wage earners for the purpose of maintaining and improving the conditions of their working lives'. What Coates and Topham have so vividly shown is the heroic and patient work that went into creating the consciousness and the supporting organisations of a Labour Movement which would guarantee that unions were indeed continuous associations.

How far, then, does such a movement of support go beyond its component parts in Trade Unions, Trades Councils, the Cooperative Societies, the Labour Party in central and local government and, at one time, including the Communist Party? How does it differ from the Women's Movement, the Peace Movement, the Green Movement? The answer must surely lie in the broad sense of a collective presence, not only of allies in times of trouble, but in a shared collective sense of being the people who make up 'our' society, whatever the masters and big-wigs might believe. For socialists it has seemed a simple class question, and for the TUC in 1898 it was natural to declare support for the 'working class parties'. Class relations, Coates and Topham remind us in reviewing the achievements of the Great Dock Strike of 1889, are 'built through interaction and are not simply self-ascribed'; and later in looking ahead from the founding of the New Unionism, they write: 'Recognition ... is a powerful reinforcement of labour solidarity, since it compels the employers to define the social world in the same terms as does the trade union ... Even when he hates it, the participating employer has sanctioned it. The organised working class ... draws strength from its adversaries, even when it is under attack. Political reform involves a wider social recognition'.

Commitment to the Labour Movement has always been a moral statement that has drawn as much from Christianity – Catholic, Protestant, non-conformist – as from Marxism, but most of all from a sense of human solidarity. It came out of a shared sense of rejection in the struggle of unions for recognition. Those who confuse recognition with incorporation have generally themselves already achieved some status in society as middle class parvenues or professionals. For those excluded from such individual upward mobility, recognition has essentially meant personal identity through a collective presence. Wages could be high or low, conditions of work better or worse, what mattered was to be recognised as a member of human society, not just as an individual only but as part of a whole community. It is still what matters for all those disadvantaged from birth and upbringing, from gender, race or religion, who in effect make up together the great majority of society.

Notes

1. Blackwells are to be congratulated on the quality of production of the book. The engravings from the Great Dock Strike, appearing as both frontispiece and cover, add much to the sense of time and place. There are only three or four typographical errors in over 800 pages, Repetition is rare in spite of the vast mass of quoted material. The long chapters are well broken up by subheadings to make reading easier. I would have liked references to ideas and themes in the index – syndicalism, industrial unions, collective bargaining, women workers etc. – as well as the names of persons and organisations and events. We have to find the Match Girls' strike under the names of their employers – Bryant and May. I found it necessary to make my own supplementary index. Perhaps in the next volumes?
2. *New Left Review,* no.167, January-February 1988

Society of Industrial Tutors' Journal